ALLEN GINSBERG

DEATH & FAME

BY ALLEN GINSBERG

POETRY

Howl and Other Poems. 1956.
Kaddish and Other Poems. 1961.
Empty Mirror: Early Poems. 1961.
Reality Sandwiches. 1963.
Planet News. 1968.
The Fall of America: Poems of These States. 1972.
The Gates of Wrath: Rhymed Poems 1948–51. 1973.
Iron Horse. 1973.
First Blues. 1975.
Mind Breaths: Poems 1971–76. 1978.
Plutonian Ode: Poems 1977–1980. 1982.
Collected Poems 1947–1980. 1984.
White Shroud: Poems 1980–1985. 1986.
Cosmopolitan Greetings: Poems 1986–1992. 1994.
Selected Poems 1947–1995. 1996.
Death & Fame: Poems 1993–1997. 1999.

PROSE

The Yage Letters (with William Burroughs). 1963.
Indian Journals. 1970, 1996.
Gay Sunshine Interview (with Allen Young). 1974.
Allen Verbatim: Lectures on Poetry, Politics, Consciousness (Gordon Ball, ed.). 1974.
The Visions of the Great Rememberer. 1974.
Chicago Trial Testimony. 1975.
To Eberhart from Ginsberg. 1976.
Journals Early Fifties Early Sixties (Gordon Ball, ed.). 1977, 1993.
As Ever: Collected Correspondence Allen Ginsberg & Neal Cassady (Barry Gifford, ed.). 1977.

Composed on the Tongue (Literary Conversations 1967–1977). 1980.
Straight Hearts Delight, Love Poems and Selected Letters 1947–1980 (with Peter Orlovsky, Winston Leyland, ed.). 1980.
Howl, Original Draft Facsimile, Fully Annotated (Barry Miles, ed.). 1986, 1995.
Journals Mid-Fifties: 1954–1958. 1994.
Luminous Dreams. 1997.

PHOTOGRAPHY

Photographs (Twelvetrees Press). 1991.
Snapshot Poetics (Michael Köhler, ed.)(Chronicle Books). 1993.

VOCAL WORDS & MUSIC

First Blues, cassette tape (Smithsonian/ Folkways FSS 37560). 1981.
Howls, Raps & Roars, 4-CD set (Fantasy). 1993.
Hydrogen Jukebox, opera with Philip Glass (Elektra Nonesuch). 1993.
Holy Soul Jelly Roll: Poems & Songs 1949–1993, 4-CD set (Rhino Records). 1994.
The Ballad of the Skeletons, with Paul McCartney and Philip Glass (Mouth Almighty/Mercury Records). 1996.
The Lion for Real (Mouth Almighty/Mercury Records). 1989, 1996.
Howl, U.S.A., Kronos Quartet, Lee Hyla score, (Nonesuch). 1996.
Howl & Other Poems (Fantasy). 1988.

ALLEN GINSBERG

DEATH & FAME

POEMS 1993–1997

Edited by Bob Rosenthal, Peter Hale, and Bill Morgan

Foreword by Robert Creeley

Afterword by Bob Rosenthal

HarperFlamingo

An Imprint of HarperCollins*Publishers*

DEATH & FAME. Copyright © 1999 by the Allen Ginsberg Trust. All rights reserved. Printed in the United States of America. No part of this book may be used or reproduced in any manner whatsoever without written permission except in the case of brief quotations embodied in critical articles and reviews. For information address HarperCollins Publishers, Inc., 10 East 53rd Street, New York, NY 10022.

HarperCollins books may be purchased for educational, business, or sales promotional use. For information please write: Special Markets Department, HarperCollins Publishers, Inc., 10 East 53rd Street, New York, NY 10022.

FIRST EDITION

Library of Congress Cataloging-in-Publication Data

Ginsberg, Allen, 1926—1997
    Death and fame : last poems, 1993—1997 / Allen Ginsberg. — 1st ed.
      p. cm.
    ISBN 0-06-019292-5
    I. Title.
  PS3513.I74D42 1999
  811' .54—dc21   98-39988

99 00 01 02 03 ❖/RRD 10 9 8 7 6 5 4 3 2 1

CONTENTS

ACKNOWLEDGMENTS

The editors wish to acknowledge the following people for their help and support: Andrew Wylie, Sarah Chalfant, Jeff Posternak, Terry Karten, Megan Barrett, Jaqueline Gens, Eliot Katz, Steven Taylor, Ben Schafer, and Regina Pellicano.

Thanks to the hospitable editors, variants of these writings were printed first in: *Aftonbladet, Allen Ginsberg e Il Saggiatore, The Alternative Press, American Poetry Review, American Sentences, Ballad of the Skeletons* [recording], *The Best American Poetry 1997, Bombay Gin, Booglit, City Lights Review, Cuaderno Carmin, Davka, Harper's* magazine, *Harvard* magazine, *Illuminated Poetics, Lettre International, Literal Latté, Long Shot, Man Alive, The Nation, New York Newsday, New York Times Book Review,* the *New Yorker, Off the Wall, Poetry Flash, Poetry Ireland Review, Shambhala Sun, Tribu, Tricycle, Viva Vine, Viva Ferlinghetti!,* and *Woodstock Journal.*

FOREWORD

Vale

This is Allen Ginsberg's last book, particular to his determining intent, his last writings when in hospital aware of his impending death, his last reflections and resolutions—his last mind. When he was told by the doctors that he had at best only a short time to live, he called his old friends to tell them the hard news, comforting, reassuring, as particular to their lives as ever. Despite the intensely demanding fame he'd had to deal with for more than forty years, he'd kept the world both intimate and transcendent. It was a "here and now" that admitted all the literal things of each day's substance and yet well knew that all such was finally "too heavy for this lightness lifts the brain into blue sky/at May dawn when birds start singing on East 12th street . . ." He was, and remains, the enduring friend, the one who goes with us wherever we are taken, who counsels and consoles, who gets the facts when it seems we will never be told them, who asks "Who'll council who lives where in the rubble,/who'll sleep in what brokenwalled hut/in the moonlight . . ." He kept a witness of impeccable kind.

The playful, reductive, teasing verses, which could sometime make this world seem just the bitter foolishness it finally has to, sound here clearly. What is the grandness of death, of a body finally worn out, at last the simple fact of stubbornly reluctant shit and a tediously malfunctioning heart, of "all the accumulations that wear us out," as he put it, when still a young man? There is no irony, no despair, in delighting as one can in "No more right & wrong/yes it's gone gone gone/ gone gone away . . ." No poet more heard, more respected, more knew the intricacies of melody's patterns. He took such pleasure in the whimsical, insistent way the very rhythms could take hold of attention, bringing each word to its singular place.

"Chopping apples into the fruit compote—suffer, suffer, suffer, suffer!" His company insisted upon music and he danced with a consummate grace.

Now we must make our own music, albeit his stays with us forever. William Blake's great call, "Hear the voice of the bard . . .," now changes to "The authors are in eternity," because ours is a passing world. Yet the heroic voices, the insistent intimacies of their tenacious humanity, hold us in a profound and securing bond. Where else would we think to live? Our friend gave his whole life to keep faith with Whitman's heartfelt insistence, "Who touches this book touches a man." So Allen Ginsberg will not leave us even now. "To see Void vast infinite look out the window into the blue sky."

Robert Creeley
June 13, 1998

DEATH
& FAME

New Democracy Wish List

for President Clinton White House

Retro Axioms:

"Progress" ended in XX century.

Hyper-rationalism reduces natural complexity of nature through narrow
thought abstraction; Hyper-rationalization, hyper-industri-
alization & Hyper-technology create chaos.

U.S. command economy subsidizes fossil fuel and nuclear Energy &
Science, Agriculture, Air & Motor Transport, Banking,
Communications, Military Industrial Complex, licit & illicit
psychoactive Drugs, also rules Mass Media via FCC . American
Free Market is hi-tech myth with national socialist central-
ized regulation implicit everywhere except small business &
little magazines.

Muscle Power connected to appropriate hi-tech might rehabilitate
Earth.

Lacks & Needs:

Fossil Fuels retard the planet. Detoxify America: tainted Fire
poisons Earth, fouls Air & pollutes Water.

Emphasize prevention & alternative medicine with medical insurance
rebates for not using Self-insured health credits: like
mythic China, "Only pay Doctor when you are well."

Fund Ryan White Care Act, separate Church & State in Center for Dis-
ease Control, fund bleach kits, needle exchange & plainspoken
AIDS education, build infrastructure of decentralized com-
munity based health care preventative medicine early inter-
vention clinics for poverty class disease-prone high-risk
teens women & men living with AIDS & TB inner city plagues.

1

Coordinate National crash program to research inexpensive anti-
     AIDS medicines.

Separate Church & State in arts, education & civil law. Restore Na-
     tional Endowment for the Arts & FCC freedom from
     Fundamentalist political intrusion.

Sexuality's loose not fixed. Legalize it.

Decriminalize addictive drug problem, doctors can cure addiction or
     provide maintenance if no cure. Reduce mass-million expense
     on narcotics-addicted political prisoners overcrowding courts
     & jails, Medicalize drug trade.

Decriminalize marijuana, its disadvantages are minor; reserve hemp
     grass as unadvertised private small cash crop for failing
     family farms, encourage hemp fabric industries.

Privatize & entrust psychedelics to medical educational priestly
     professions. End Military monopoly on LSD research and
     development.

End tobacco farming subsidies, cut use. Ex-Nicotine lobbyists working
     in Clinton's new White House can stop smoking.

Shift agricultural subsidies toward grain beans & vegetable diet. Tax
     meat as a nutritional agronomic & ecologic disaster.

With massive scale reforestation rural & in wilderness, plant also uni-
     versal urban tree rows.

Establish Civilian Conservation Corps for Urban homesteading, thin out
     corrupt local bureaucracies obstructing populist housing re-
     construction.

Encourage international trade in Eco-technology in place of enabling
     codependency on weapons trade.

Inaugurate National "Limits of Growth" Program for Population/Land
Use/Pollution.

Jump start national state & city human and industrial waste compost &
recycling.

Honor primary and secondary school teachers, elevate respect, reward
educators as handsomely as Plumbers, reduce class crowding to
human size, under 15 students; encourage national child-care
projects.

Take back money from SLA bankruptcy profiteer goniffs.

Purge U.S. military death squad subsidies in Salvador, Guatemala, etc.
We backed up dictators in Zaire, Somalia, Liberia, Sudan,
Angola, Haiti, Iran, Iraq, Salvador, we're responsible: admit
it then figure ways out.

Open CIA & FBI & NSA archives on Cointelpro raids, Government drug
dealing, Kennedy/King assassinations, Iranian Contragate,
Panama Deception, Vatican, Hand & Lavoro Bank thuggery, etc.
including Bush-Noriega relations and other CIA client-agent
scandals.

Open all secret files on J. Edgar Hoover-Cardinal Spellman-Roy Cohn-
Joe McCarthy alcoholic Closet-Queen Conspiracy with Organized
Crime to sabotage the U.S. Labor Movement, Native African-
American Hispanic & Gay minority leaderships; and blackmail
U.S. Presidents Congress each other for half century.

Get Government Secret Police (DEA CIA FBI NSA etc.) off our backs by
the next millennium.

January 17, 1993

Peace in Bosnia-Herzegovina

General Mother Teresa
   Emperor Dalai Lama XIV
      Chief of Staff Thich Nhat Hanh
        Army Chaplain John Paul II
followed by the shades of Gandhi
   Sakharov, Sartre & his uncle
         Albert Schweitzer
went to the bombed out streets
talked to Moslem Bosnians in
   the burnt out grocery stores
parlayed with Croatian & Serbian Generals & Parliament
asked them to quit shooting & firing
   artillery from the mountainside
overlooking villages
   emptied of grandmothers—
So now there was quiet—a few fires
   smoldered in back alleys
a few corpses stank in wet fields
—But who owns these houses? The
   cinema theaters with broken doors?
Who owns that grocery store, that City Hall,
   that windowless school with broken
   rooftiles?
Who owns these little apartments, now
   all worshippers of Allah
pray in towns besieged 100 miles away
overcrowded in tenements & tents, with
   U.N. portosans at the crossroads?
Who owns these abandoned alleys &
   drugstores with shattered bottle shards over
   the sidewalk & inside the door?
Who'll be the judge, attorney, file
   legal briefs,

bankruptcy papers, affidavits of ownership,
      deeds, old tax receipts?
Who'll council who lives where in the rubble,
      who'll sleep in what brokenwalled hut
in the full moonlight when spring clouds
      pass over the face
of the man in the moon at the end of May?

May 6, 1993, 3 A.M.

After the Party

amid glasses clinking, mineral water, schnapps
among professors' smiling beards,
sneaker'd classicists, intelligent lady millionaire
       literary Patron fag hags
       earth mothers of Lambeth, Trocadero,
       Hyde Park, 5th Avenue
blond haired journalists with bracelets, grand
       readers of Dostojevsky & Gogol—
senior editor escorts from Trotskyite weeklies,
lesbians sitting on glossy magazine covers—
what have we here? a kid moving from
       foyer to bathroom, thin body,
Pale cheeked with red cap, 18 year old window washer,
       came with Señora Murillo
She admired his impudence, amused by his
       sincere legs
as I admire his glance, he turns aside to
       gaze at me, I'm
happy to guess he'll show his
       naked body in bed
where we talk the refined old doctrine,
       Coemergent Wisdom

                  Lódź, October 5, 1993
       9:15 P.M. at "Construction in Process" poetry reading

After Olav H. Hauge

I

Some live on islands, hills near Trondheim
Some in St. Moritz, or the forest depths
Some lonely have beautiful wives
castles, fine carpets on Wall Street
Buy & sell currencies, solitary on marble floors
consumed by a passion for fossil fuel
magnetized by cannons, lasers, bombsights, enriched uranium
or together play the stock market
They live & die at the throw of the dice
They're all businessmen
who have found eachother.

II
Fermented Jungle

North wind blows
Fish fly around the room
wind dies down
Fish fly under water.

III

Sometimes the Godliness
          strikes me as heroic
People mill about
Bodø won the Norwegian soccer cup
It's so crowded, fans are drunk
Peoples' feet get mixed up
That big man wanders around
                    lost, barefoot
he can't find his feet—
Finally he goes out, late
on his way home
not sure if he's on
his own two feet

Trondheim, October 25, 1993

These knowing age

These knowing age
fart
These knowing age
walk slowly
these knowing age
remind themselves of their grandmothers
these knowing age
take waterpills, high blood pressure,
        watch their sugar and salt
these knowing age eat less meat, some
        stopped smoking a decade ago
Some quit coffee, some drink it strong
These knowing age saw
best friends' funerals, telephoned
        daughters & granddaughters
Some drive, some don't, some cook, some
        do not
These knowing age often
keep quiet.

Munich, November 5, 1993

C'mon Pigs of Western Civilization Eat More Grease

Eat Eat more marbled Sirloin more Pork'n
        gravy!
Lard up the dressing, fry chicken in
        boiling oil
Carry it dribbling to gray climes, snowed with
        salt,
Little lambs covered with mint roast in racks
        surrounded by roast potatoes wet with
        buttersauce,
Buttered veal medallions in creamy saliva,
        buttered beef, by glistening mountains
        of french fries
Stroganoffs in white hot sour cream, chops
        soaked in olive oil,
surrounded by olives, salty feta cheese, followed
        by Roquefort & Bleu & Stilton
        thirsty
for wine, beer Cocacola Fanta Champagne
        Pepsi retsina arak whiskey vodka
Agh! Watch out heart attack, pop more
        angina pills
order a plate of Bratwurst, fried frankfurters,
couple billion Wimpys', McDonald's burgers
        to the moon & burp!
Salt on those fries! Hot dogs! Milkshakes!
Forget greenbeans, everyday a few carrots,
        a mini big spoonful of salty rice'll
        do, make the plate pretty;
throw in some vinegar pickles, briny sauerkraut
        check yr. cholesterol, swallow a pill
and order a sugar Cream donut, pack 2 under
        the size 44 belt
Pass out in the vomitorium come back cough
        up strands of sandwich still chewing
        pastrami at Katz's delicatessen

Back to central Europe & gobble Kielbasa
        in Lódź
swallow salami in Munich with beer, Liverwurst
on pumpernickel in Berlin, greasy cheese in
        a 3 star Hotel near Syntagma, on white
        bread thick-buttered
Set an example for developing nations, salt,
        sugar, animal fat, coffee tobacco Schnapps
Drop dead faster! make room for
        Chinese guestworkers with alien soybean
        curds green cabbage & rice!
Africans Latins with rice beans & calabash can
        stay thin & crowd in apartments for working
        class foodfreaks—

Not like Western cuisine rich in protein
        cancer heart attack hypertension sweat
        bloated liver & spleen megaly
Diabetes & stroke—monuments to carnivorous
        civilizations
presently murdering Belfast
        Bosnia Cypress Ngorno Karabach Georgia
mailing love letter bombs in
        Vienna or setting houses afire
        in East Germany—have another coffee,
        here's a cigar.
And this is a plate of black forest chocolate cake,
        you deserve it.

Athens, December 19, 1993

Here We Go 'Round the Mulberry Bush

I got old & shit in my pants
　　　　　shit in my pants
　　　　　shit in my pants
I got old & shit in my pants
　　　　　shit in my pants again

We got old & shit in our pants
　　　　　shit in our pants
　　　　　shit in our pants
We got old & shit in our pants
　　　　　shit in our pants again

You'll be lucky if you get old
　　　　　& shit in your pants
　　　　　& shit in your pants
You'll be lucky if you get old
　　　　　& shit in your pants again

January 1, 1994

Tuesday Morn

Waking with aching back at base of spine, walked stiffly to kitchen
        toilet to pee,
more limber returned to unmade bed, sat to write, dreamlike yesterdays
        recorded—
From pill dispenser 60 mg Lasix, water pills brings blood to kidney to
        relieve heart stressed by lung liquid
one white Lanoxin something further steadies the heart, one brown
        Vasotec for high blood pressure
a round blue potassium pill set aside for breakfast
Next another quaff of water for sleep-dried tongue
& check stove water boiling Tibetan medical powders
Quarter tsp. directly in mouth with hot water, morn & night
Next make the bed—pull out mattress, lift up sheets ballooning in air
        to settle all four corners,
lay on the orange-diamonded Mexican wool blanket & 3 pillows—
        push mattress back in place
brush teeth—then prick my finger
a drop, Exac-Tech blood sugar teststrip results noted morn & eve
98 today, a little low, swab pinkie with alcohol pad, another sip medi-
        cinal tea—
replace reading glasses with bifocals, brush teeth at front-room sink
        & looking out window, church door passers-by four floors
        below
while noon bells ring, clock ticking on the kitchen wall above the toilet
        cabinet—pull chain
worked this morning, flushed a wobbly porcelain throne—needa get
        Mike the Super fix pipes—
Back to front room, brush teeth, bowels begin to stir relief, electric
        shave,
brush out gray dust from razor head, wash face, clear throat's pale yellow
        phlegm, blow nose
in paper towel, stick pinkie end with white cream Borofax drop in
        each nostril, wipe mustache, put on teashirt
Vitalis on short hair around bald head, brush back small beard—&
        ready for breakfast

in boxer shorts alone at home, pee again, gray sky out window
Sparrows on courtyard dirt, bare Heaven Trees—yesterday's *Times*
        half read on the table where
red tulip blossoms dry in a glass jar—Time to crap & finish *Exquisite*
        Corpse—not much came down—
flush, climb ladder and fix the water ball, wash ass change shorts and
        choose fresh sox—
At last it's time to eat, clear & safe in the morning—1 P.M.
Salt-free cornflakes from the icebox, brown rice, shredded wheat in a
        Chinese bowl
filled thereafter with Rice Dream milk—banana that!
Chew and wonder what to read, answer phone, yes, "Peter's flown to
        Colorado, Huncke's rent is due" to patron Hiro—
Finish cereal reading yesterday's *Times* "How Mental Patients Sleep
        Out of Doors"
" 'Last time, I was just walking in the rain,' he said, his hands and lips
        quivering slightly from the medication he takes."
Slip a multivitamin pill in my mouth, grab a dish, fruit stewed two
        nites ago—
Ring Ring the telephone—the office, Bob Rosenthal, Debbie for Jewel
        Heart Benefit,
Ysrael Lubavitcher fairy returned from his Paris year
Edith not home, Aunt Honey leaving for Australia next week,
she had stroke & splenectomy 1942, long story—
David Rome preparing arts program Halifax during Sawang's Shambhala
        confirmation
—Finally 3 P.M. I get dressed go to office couple hours—
Phone Robert Frank? Yup, he's out, call early evening. I'm free.

                                     January 23, 1994

God

The 18 year old marine "had made his Peace with God."
A word. A capitol G. Who is God? I thought I saw him once
and heard his voice, which now sounds like my own,
and I'm not God, so who's God? Jesus Bible God?
Whose Bible? Old JHVH? The 4 letter one without vowels or the 3 letter
        word God? G-O-D?
Allah? Some say Allah's great, tho' mock his name you're dead!
Zoroaster's Wise One used to be great, & Mormons' version got
        absolute pedigrees & Genealogies.
Is Pope's God same as Southern Baptist Inerrancy televangelists?
How's that square with the Ayatollah's Allah, Billy Graham Nixon's on
        his knees, Ronald Reagan's Armageddon deity?
What of Lubavitcher Rabbi's God refusing land for peace exchange?
Is Yassir Arafat's God same as Shamir's? What about Magna Mater?
What happened to Aphrodite, Hecate, Diana many breasted at Ephesus,
round bottom'd Willendorf Venus older than Jahweh & Allah &
        Zoroaster's dream!
older than Confucius, Lao Tzu, Buddha & the 39 patriarchs.
Is any God real? Is there one God? How come so many Gods—
Fighting eachother, poor Mayans, Aztecs, Peruvian sun worshippers?
        Hopi peyote dreamers round the half moon fire.
Am I God after all, made the universe, we dreamed it up together
or got tumbled out of the Chute onto the Planet, looking for progenitors?
I know I'm not God, are you? Don't be silly.
God? God? Everybody's God? Don't be silly.

February 25, 1994

Ah War

Ah War bigness addiction
Alchemized thru meta-industrial
Labor-Intensive permanent tree
Crop protein energy system
recycling Urban Wastes
in Meditative Egoless non
Theistic Space

Lisner Auditorium
Monday, March 21, 1994, 8:00 P.M.

Excrement

Everybody excretes different loads
To think of it—
Marilyn Monroe's pretty buttocks,
                    Eleanor Roosevelt's bloomers dropt
            Rudolf Valentino on the seat, taut
                        muscles relaxing
Presidents looking down the bowl
                        to see their state of health
            Our White House rosy-cheeked dieter,
                One last, gaunt sourpuss
                    striped pants ankle'd
                        in the Water Chamber

Name it? byproduct of
                vegetables, steak, sausages, rice
            reduced to a brown loaf in the watery tureen,
                        splatter of dark mud on highway
                    side cornfields
            studded with peanuts & grape seeds—

Who doesn't attend to her business
No matter nobility, Hollywood starshine, media
                Blitz-heroics, everyone at
                    table follows watercloset
                        regulation & relief
An empty feeling going back to banquet,
                returned to bed, sitting for Breakfast,
            a pile of dirt unloaded from gut level
                mid-belly, down thru the butthole
                        relaxed & released from the ton
                            of old earth, poured back
                                    on Earth

It never appears in public
   'cept cartoons, filthy canards,
      political commix left & right
The Eminent Cardinal his robes pushed aside,
    Empress of Japan her 60 pound kimono,
      layered silks pushed aside,
The noble German Statesman giving his heart ease
    The pretty student boy in Heidelberg
      between chemic processor abstractions,
Keypunch operators in vast newsrooms
        Editors their wives and children
    drop feces of various colors
     iron supplement black
      to pale green-white sausage
      delicacies the same
       in tiny bathroom
        distant suburbs,
   even dogs on green front lawns
      produce their simulacra of
      human garbage
    we all drop
Myself the poet aging on the stool
  Polyhymnia the Muse herself, lowered to this throne—
    what a relief!

March 24, 1994

New Stanzas for *Amazing Grace*

I dreamed I dwelled in a homeless place
Where I was lost alone
Folk looked right through me into space
And passed with eyes of stone

O homeless hand on many a street
Accept this change from me
A friendly smile or word is sweet
As fearless charity

Woe workingman who hears the cry
And cannot spare a dime
Nor look into a homeless eye
Afraid to give the time

So rich or poor no gold to talk
A smile on your face
The homeless ones where you may walk
Receive amazing grace

I dreamed I dwelled in a homeless place
Where I was lost alone
Folk looked right through me into space
And passed with eyes of stone

April 2, 1994

Composed at the request of Ed Sanders for his production of The New Amaz-
ing Grace, performed November 20, 1994, at the Poetry Project in St. Mark's
Church in-the-Bouwerie.

City Lights City

On Via Ferlinghetti & Kerouac Alley young heroes muse melancholy
    2025 A.D.
Musicians brood & pace Bob Kaufman Street and practice future jazz
    on Rexroth place
Spiritual novelists sit rapt in contemplation under the street sign at
    Saroyan Place before they cross to Aram Alley
Loves' eyes gaze sparkling on Bay waters from McClure Plaza at the
    foot of Market
Old Market itself as Robert Duncan Boulevard teems with theosophic
    shops & Hermetic Department Stores
& crossing Duncan Blvd.: First DiPrima Second Henry Miller Third
    Corso Street
Fourth Jeffers Street & Fifth on John Wieners Street the Greyhound
    Terminal stands
surrounded by Bookstore Galleries, Publishers Rows, and Artists lofts
Sightseers in tourist buses breathe fresh foggy air on Harold Norse &
    Hirschman Peaks—oldies but goldies
Ken Kesey's name makes Bayshore famous as you barrel up past
    Brother Everson Memorial Stadium
Whalen Bridge sits meditating all the way to Oakland
Snyder Bridge connects the East-West Gate between S.F. & Marin
Commuters crowd exhausted into the Neal Cassady R.R. Station on
    Corso
Czeslaw Milosz Street signs shine bright on Van Ness
Poet Jack Micheline gets Tenderloin, Philip Lamantia Tower crowns
    Telegraph Hill
where international surrealist tourists climb to see the view—
& I'll take Alcatraz (to return to Native Americans along with Treasure
    Island)

April 21, 1994

Newt Gingrich Declares War on "McGovernik Counterculture"

Does that mean war on every boy with more than one earring on the
        same ear?
against every girl with a belly button ring? What about nose piercing?
        a diamond in right nostril?
Does that mean more plainclothesmen high on LSD at Dead concerts?
What about MTV—no more Michael Jackson, no Dylan Subterranean
        Homesick Blues? Yoko & John no more Give Peace a Chance
Will there be laws against Punk, Generation X, the Voidoids, Slackers,
        Grunge?
Blues, Jazz, Bebop, Rocknroll? Where did it get countercultural?
What about Elvis' Pelvis? Sonic Youth dumbed, Cobain's screams
        banished from Nirvana?
No more grass on college campuses, Mushrooms stomped to death by
        the Elephant Party?
What about African-Americans? That's a terrific Counterculture, &
        what about the Yellow Peril, Chinese restaurants? New Age
        Cooking? is Japanese Sushi too much Zen?
Sitting meditation, that be frowned satanic in Congress? Tai Chi, Tai
        Kwando, Karate, Martial Arts? Ballet? Opera, *La Bohème*?
Don't mention us cocksuckers?! Is eating pussy countercultural?
        Sappho, Socrates, Da Vinci, Shakespeare, Michelangelo,
        Proust in or out the canon?
J. E. Hoover's name wiped off FBI granite in the Capital?
Poetry slams, is poetry countercultural, like a Third Party?
Is ecology pro or counter culture? Astronomy determining the Uni-
        verse's age & size?
Long hair, relativity, is Einstein countercultural?

January 1995

Pastel Sentences (Selections)

Mice ate at the big red heart in her breast, she was distracted in
      love.

Bowed down by the weight of nebulae he crouches underneath the
      hill.

A bat that's bigger than your ear watches you sleep while you dream
      him there.

A round blue eye woke red lipped 'neath this century's gigantic lightbulb.

Lantern-jawed Bismarck dreams a rich red rose blossoms thorn-
      stemmed through his skull.

In an oval blue womb a full-grown girl curled up eyes closed dreams
      her birth.

Big little people do yab yum in their ten petal'd yellow daisy.

Long hand over left eye Mother Sudan sees big bellied kids' thin
      ribs.

In midst of coition a blood-red worm spurts out his heaving rib-
      cage.

The one eyed moon-whale watches you weep, drifting brown seas in
      a pale boat.

Thirty Kingdoms' keys chainmailed down his chest, the Pope dreams
      he's St. Peter.

Jeannie Duval's cheek tickled by a Paris fly, 1852.

Puff a cigarette between skullfleshed lips, smoke gets in your empty
eyes.

Sphincter-wound in his chest, he kneels and lifts both hands in
surprise to pray.

All mixed up breasts feet genitals nipples & hands, both fall into
sleep.

Adam contemplates his navel covered with a bush of jealous hearts.

Body spread open, black legs held down, she eats his ice cream—white
sex-tongue.

One centaur palm raised thru earth-crust lifts a red live dog barking
at stars.

Her dog licks the live red heart of th' African lady curled up in bed.

Naked in solitary prison cell he looks down at a hard-on.

Hands hold her ass tight with joy to lick & eat the blue star 'twixt her
thighs.

Small pink-winged Lady-Heart hovers, rose-cunt legs spread nigh his
stiff black dick.

Chic shoes rest in a black rose vortex of sociable fashion money.

She poses self-confident, blue sky & clouds borne in her oval womb.

Lady Buddha sleeps on blue air in a green leaf, knees raised spread
naked.

Repose open-eyed on starry blue pillows under a star-roofed sky.

The black guy steps in the shade, glancing back at the sunlit boy he
screwed.

Legs behind neck, arms hung down, Yogi's solar anal navel burns
   red.

Blowing bubbles in blue sky he squats on his own blue bubble planet.

Star, bird, cane & big thigh bones, the ghost baby dreams life
   beyond the womb.

Regarding their long thick tails, blue demons wrestle with golden
   scissors.

He steps on his own breast lying in bed with red half hard-on.

Lady snails delicately climb naked thighs to stir his genitals.

Left forefinger probed into his own left hand proves a Doubting
   Thomas.

They exchange glances, a bee shadows her tail, a rose grows on his
   hip.

William Burroughs' skeleton twists a towel, he's got the bloody rag
   on.

The rose-girl kneels weighed down, iron tanks on shoulder, coccyx,
   calves & footsoles.

Horse stands on horse upon horse, lie back on top & take your forty
   winks.

He dives from naked sky past the sun's nimbus into space-blue ocean.

Curtains part on a nail and its shadow, Samsara's drama Act I.

The red lip'd fat billionaire appeals you try out his wee twat or dick.

Arms to neck, his tit, her belly, prong-twat, the President and his
   wife.

Pale green headless phantoms upside-down dipsy-doodle with thin
      hard-ons.

Lady Day bows her neck under a pyramid of oily black rocks.

Beneath breast-eyed wasp-beaks the pink rose opens, better get in
      there quick!

Inside her red womb the hermaphrodite fetus closes a third eye.

Wiping blood-black tears from hard labor, try holding up your
      big sad head.

Jealousy! Jealousy! Chin in hand he ponders the Unfaithful Muse.

Young Don Juan bravely displays his girlish red-sexed lips and
      eyeshadow.

Caught in the burning house of my brown body I fainted openeyed.

Big phallus, black womb lined with reddish flesh, look at the monkey
      we birthed.

One bird pecks her double's breast on a ghost-white lingam's
      unblinking head.

She flies down thousands of stone steps for years, aged climbs them
      all back up.

for Francesco Clemente
Château Chenonceau, June 24, 1995
Naropa Institute, July 5, 1995
Lawrence, Kansas, July 22, 1995

Nazi Capish

Catholicism capish
Catholicism capish
Catholicism abortion capish
Capish capish capish

Christian capish
Christian capish
Christian sin capish

Islamic capish
Islamic capish
Islamic Jihad capish

Zionist capish
Zionist capish
Zionist nationalist capish

Fundamentalism capish
Fundamentalism capish
Fundamentalism absolutism
Fundamentalism capish

Hunkie Honkie Aryan Frog
Jap & Gook & Limey Wog
        Afric Chink capish

Nazi capish
Nazi capish
Nazi capish capish

Commie capish
Commie capish
Commie capish capish

Capitalist capish
Capitalist capish
Capitalist capish capish

Fascisti capish
Fascisti capish
Fascisti shit capish

September 21, 1995

Is About

Dylan is about the Individual against the whole of creation
Beethoven is about one man's fist in the lightning clouds
The Pope is about abortion & the spirits of the dead . . .
Television is about people sitting in their living room looking at their
       things
America is about being a big Country full of Cowboys Indians Jews
       Negroes & Americans
Orientals Chicanos Factories skyscrapers Niagara Falls Steel Mills
       radios homeless Conservatives, don't forget
Russia is about Tzars Stalin Poetry Secret Police Communism barefoot
       in the snow
But that's not really Russia it's a concept
A concept is about how to look at the earth from the moon
without ever getting there. The moon is about love & Werewolves, also
       Poe.
Poe is about looking at the moon from the sun
or else the graveyard
Everything is about something if you're a thin movie producer chain-
       smoking muggles
The world is about overpopulation, Imperial invasions, Biocide,
       Genocide, Fratricidal Wars, Starvation, Holocaust, mass
       injury & murder, high technology
Super science, atom Nuclear Neutron Hydrogen detritus, Radiation
       Compassion Buddha, Alchemy
Communication is about monopoly television radio movie newspaper
       spin on Earth, i.e. planetary censorship.
Universe is about Universe.
Allen Ginsberg is about confused mind writing down newspaper
       headlines from Mars—
The audience is about salvation, the listeners are about sex, Spiritual
       gymnastics, nostalgia for the Steam Engine & Pony Express
Hitler Stalin Roosevelt & Churchill are about arithmetic & Quadri-
       lateral equations, above all chemistry physics & chaos theory—

Who cares what it's all about?
I do! Edgar Allan Poe cares! Shelley cares! Beethoven & Dylan care.
Do you care? What are you about
or are you a human being with 10 fingers & two eyes?

New York City,
October 24, 1995

The Ballad of the Skeletons

Said the Presidential Skeleton
I won't sign the bill
Said the Speaker skeleton
Yes you will

Said the Representative Skeleton
I object
Said the Supreme Court skeleton
Whaddya expect

Said the Military skeleton
Buy Star Bombs
Said the Upperclass Skeleton
Starve unmarried moms

Said the Yahoo Skeleton
Stop dirty art
Said the Right Wing skeleton
Forget about yr heart

Said the Gnostic Skeleton
The Human Form's divine
Said the Moral Majority skeleton
No it's not it's mine

Said the Buddha Skeleton
Compassion is wealth
Said the Corporate skeleton
It's bad for your health

Said the Old Christ skeleton
Care for the Poor
Said the Son of God skeleton
AIDS needs cure

Said the Homophobe skeleton
Gay folk suck
Said the Heritage Policy skeleton
Blacks're outa luck

Said the Macho skeleton
Women in their place
Said the Fundamentalist skeleton
Increase human race

Said the Right-to-Life skeleton
Foetus has a soul
Said Pro Choice skeleton
Shove it up your hole

Said the Downsized skeleton
Robots got my job
Said the Tough-on-Crime skeleton
Tear gas the mob

Said the Governor skeleton
Cut school lunch
Said the Mayor skeleton
Eat the budget crunch

Said the Neo Conservative skeleton
Homeless off the street!
Said the Free Market skeleton
Use 'em up for meat

Said the Think Tank skeleton
Free Market's the way
Said the S&L skeleton
Make the State pay

Said the Chrysler skeleton
Pay for you & me
Said the Nuke Power skeleton
& me & me & me

Said the Ecologic skeleton
Keep Skies blue
Said the Multinational skeleton
What's it worth to you?

Said the NAFTA skeleton
Get rich, Free Trade,
Said the Maquiladora skeleton
Sweat shops, low paid

Said the rich GATT skeleton
One world, high tech
Said the Underclass skeleton
Get it in the neck

Said the World Bank skeleton
Cut down your trees
Said the I.M.F. skeleton
Buy American cheese

Said the Underdeveloped skeleton
Send me rice
Said Developed Nations' skeleton
Sell your bones for dice

Said the Ayatollah skeleton
Die writer die
Said Joe Stalin's skeleton
That's no lie

Said the Middle Kingdom skeleton
We swallowed Tibet
Said the Dalai Lama skeleton
Indigestion's whatcha get

Said the World Chorus skeleton
That's their fate
Said the USA skeleton
Gotta save Kuwait

Said the Petrochemical skeleton
Roar Bombers roar!
Said the Psychedelic skeleton
Smoke a dinosaur

Said Nancy's skeleton
Just say No
Said the Rasta skeleton
Blow Nancy Blow

Said Demagogue skeleton
Don't smoke Pot
Said Alcoholic skeleton
Let your liver rot

Said the Junkie skeleton
Can't we get a fix?
Said the Big Brother skeleton
Jail the dirty pricks

Said the Mirror skeleton
Hey good looking
Said the Electric Chair skeleton
Hey what's cooking?

Said the Talkshow skeleton
Fuck you in the face
Said the Family Values skeleton
My family values mace

Said the N.Y. Times skeleton
That's not fit to print
Said the C.I.A. skeleton
Cantcha take a hint?

Said the Network skeleton
Believe my lies
Said the Advertising skeleton
Don't get wise!

Said the Media skeleton
Believe you Me
Said the Couch-potato skeleton
What me worry?

Said the TV skeleton
Eat sound bites
Said the Newscast skeleton
That's all Goodnight

February 12–16, 1995

"You know what I'm saying?"

I was shy and tender as a 10 year old kid, you know what I'm saying?
Afraid people'd find me out in Eastside H.S. locker room you know
        what I'm saying?
Earl had beautiful hips & biceps when he took off his clothes to put on
        gym shorts you know what I'm saying?
His nose was too long, his face like a ferret but his white body
Proportioned thin, muscular definition thighs & breasts, with boy's
        nipples you know what I'm saying? uncircumcised
& strange, goyishe beauty you know what I'm saying, I was dumb-
        struck—
at Golden 50th H.S. Reunion I recognized him, bowed, & exchanged
        pleasant words, you know what I'm saying?
He was retired, wife on his arm, you know what I'm saying?
& Millie Peller "The Class Whore" warmest woman at our last Silver
        25th Reunion alas had passed away
She was nice to me a scared gay kid at Eastside High, you know what
        I'm saying?

December 23, 1995

34

Bowel Song

You've been coughing for weeks
still you don't sit on your cushion & visualize Bam
You've been in the hospital just last week
still you read the newspapers
Recovered from congestive heart failure,
you took 7 hours last week to read the Sunday N.Y. Times
Listen, your days are numbered, why waste the essence of your clock
How will you feel when you can't breathe?
What'll you do the last six minutes?
Where'll you go for the next 6 hours
What good, half dozen gay porno films then?
You can hardly catch your breath now, why jack off limp prick?
Your master gives good advice, you listen, follow it couple weeks
then lapse into old habits, waste time on the toilet reading books,
at the kitchen sink 3am washing dishes daydreaming.
If you don't get ready now, what'll you do at the Black Hole
You wanna get born a pretty little girl & go through agony?
Wanna get caught between snakes coupling?
In between death and life, still wanna get laid?
What makes you lazy? you're not on your deathbed yet,
if you've an ounce of strength, use it to look inside.
Clear your mind, you won't escape the Great Sickness
the Immortal Plague, Grand Disaster continuous to eternity—
Whatever it is, whyn'cha figure it out?
Wanna drift off & become a newspaper headline,
what good favorable publicity in the bardo?
Allen Ginsberg says, these words'll get you nowhere
these jokes won't be funny when everyone leaves the seven exits.

January 2, 1996

Popular Tunes

What do I hear in my ear
        approaching my 70th year—
Echoes of popular tunes, old rhymes
             familiar runes
Songs my mother taught me
       "O tell me pretty maiden
          are there any more at home
              like you?"
Cousin Claire heard on the Newark radio
Aunt Elanor played on her Bronx phonograph
piercing Bell Song soprano notes,
        sostenuto Amelita Galli-Curci & Rosa Ponselle
Wind up Victrola Yiddish Monologues
    Cohen On The Telephone,
        The Wind the Wind,
"Last night da vind, da vind blew down da shutters."
      "No I didn't say shuddup!"
The fugitive words of a Scots contralto
    woman's chant "McCushla,
   McCushla my dark eyed McCushla"
Ask Aunt Honey age 83, ask Stepmother Edith just 90,
    they'll know—
      they'll remember
"The March of the Wooden Soldiers," tin drums
    & pipes of *Babes in Toyland*
"Comin' thru the rye" new generations of
    folksing kids never remember sung
when they play Guitar on Union Square's
      L train subway platform—
or "Auchichornya, auchimolinka, rasdrivyminya,
    molijeninka," with Mandolins or Balalaikas
and "Tis the last rose of Summer" by Thomas Moore—
    echoing thru Time's skull as my beard's
      turned white, sugar high in my blood
        coughing weeks on end fall to winter,

Chronic bronchitis the rest of my days?
& "Down will come baby cradle and all"
        as 1930's all fell down with
        mournful Peat Bog Soldiers'
            "Lied des Concentrationslagers"

February 9, 1996

Five A.M.

Élan that lifts me above the clouds
into pure space, timeless, yea eternal
Breath transmitted into words
             Transmuted back to breath
        in one hundred two hundred years
nearly Immortal, Sappho's 26 centuries
of cadenced breathing—beyond time, clocks, empires, bodies, cars,
chariots, rocket ships skyscrapers, Nation empires
brass walls, polished marble, Inca Artwork
of the mind—but where's it come from?
Inspiration? The muses drawing breath for you? God?
Nah, don't believe it, you'll get entangled in Heaven or Hell—
Guilt power, that makes the heart beat wake all night
flooding mind with space, echoing thru future cities, Megalopolis or
Cretan village, Zeus' birth cave Lassithi Plains—Otsego County
           farmhouse, Kansas front porch?
Buddha's a help, promises ordinary mind no nirvana—
coffee, alcohol, cocaine, mushrooms, marijuana, laughing gas?
Nope, too heavy for this lightness lifts the brain into blue sky
at May dawn when birds start singing on East 12th street—
Where does it come from, where does it go forever?

May 1996

Power

The N Power, the feminine power
    the woman power the
    flower power, the power of Marigolds
    & roses, Sequoia power,
    Nature's power
wont blossom in this lifetime
    or the next, this Yuga's finished,
    seeds shot, entered the earth
    gestating with alligators & waterworms
    in swamps where planes crash,
Next lifetimes after, watch roses turn
    red, Marigolds yellow, little
    sequoias begin to climb the sky
Millions of African kids'll grow up
    amid green bushes & radiant
        camelopards again—
Down 12th Street corner Avenue A midnight police
    lean against Bodega shutters looking for
    last week's swarthy crack pushers

May 15, 1996, 11 A.M.

Anger

How'd I get angry? Analytic approach:
M'I still angry with Carolyn? forty three years ago
       kicked me out of bed with
          naked Neal their house San Jose—
Disadvantaged hating Podhoretz
       for put-down of Beat writers
          queers nineteen fifty eight
       later defense of death-squad drug-dealer
        Generals in El Salvador
          & op-ed B2 Bombers
Angrily sat an hour adamant
       Thangka-thief meth-head Gaiton's apt.
        E. Houston Street nineteen sixty three
          never got my Dancing Skeletons back—
Never forgave late Alan Marlowe nineteen seventy five
       stole back my $100 loan gift
       to Jyoti Datta Calcutta four years earlier
Lost my telephone temper with critic Walter
       Goodman
       insulting Gunther Grass' visit to poor South Bronx
International PEN Congress nineteen eighty five
       & my own handmade Nicaraguan
       Contra-War peace petition mocked
          as "all the news that's fit to print."

May 18, 1996

Multiple Identity Questionnaire

"Nature empty, everything's pure;
Naturally pure, that's what I am."

I'm a jew? a nice Jewish boy?
A flaky Buddhist, certainly
Gay in fact pederast? I'm exaggerating?
Not only queer an amateur S&M fan, someone should spank me for
      saying that
Columbia Alumnus class of '48, Beat icon, students say.
White, if jews are "white race"
American by birth, passport, and residence
Slavic heritage, mama from Vitebsk, father's forebears Grading in
      Kamenetz-Podolska near Lvov.
I'm an intellectual! Anti-intellectual, anti-academic
Distinguished Professor of English Brooklyn College,
Manhattanite, Another middle class liberal,
but lower class second generation immigrant,
Upperclass, I own a condo loft, go to art gallery Buddhist Vernissage
      dinner parties with Niarchos, Rockefellers, and Luces
Oh what a sissy, Professor Four-eyes, can't catch a baseball or drive a
      car—courageous Shambhala Graduate Warrior
addressed as "Maestro" Milano, Venezia, Napoli
Still student, chela, disciple, my guru Gelek Rinpoche,
Senior Citizen, got Septuagenarian discount at Alfalfa's Healthfoods
      New York subway—
Mr. Sentient Being!—Absolutely empty neti neti identity, Maya Nobo-
      daddy, relative phantom nonentity

July 5, 1996, Naropa Tent,
Boulder, CO

Don't Get Angry with Me

for Chödok Tulku

Don't get angry with me
You might die tomorrow
I'm an empty hungry ghost
Any spare change I can borrow?

Don't get angry with me
Full of God tomorrow
Could get sorry you got mad,
wanna be the God of sorrow?

Don't get angry with me
War starts tomorrow
I'll get bombed You'll get shot
in the eye with Interdependent Arrow

Don't get angry with me
Hell's hot tomorrow
If we're burned up now inflamed
Could pass aeons in cold horror

Don't get angry with me
We'll be worms tomorrow
Both wriggling in the mud
cut in two by the ploughman's harrow

Don't get angry with me—
Who'll we be tomorrow?
who knows who we are today?
Better meditate & pray,
          Tila, Mila, Marpa, Naro.

August 27, 1996

Swan Songs in the Present

"Swan songs in the present
moon systems in gleeps
Don't hang on to the essence
the refrigerator's for keeps
the Hot house vernacular
Sets up on the moldy hill
you and I climb the ribcage
& look for a heart to kill

you can do whatcha want with Europe
Eat Bananas with your dung
Whistle while you wonk the Pope
Breathe out of a spastic lung
but you'll live forever anyway
in birds' beasts hungry ghosts
& various Boddhisattvas
Drinking morning coffee
eating loxes & toasts

Hypnogogi Twaddle
anytime I can
But 70 years I'll sleep
like other old men

October 29, 1996, 3:50 A.M.

Gone Gone Gone

*"The wan moon is sinking under the white wave
and time is sinking with me, O!"*

—*Robert Burns*

yes it's gone gone gone
gone gone away
yes it's gone gone gone
gone gone away
yes it's gone gone gone
gone gone away
yes it's gone gone gone
it's all gone away
gone gone gone
won't be back today
gone gone gone
just like yesterday
gone gone gone
isn't any more
gone to the other shore
gone gone gone
it wasn't here to stay
yes it's gone gone gone
all gone out to play
yes it's gone gone gone
until another day
no one here to pray
gone gone gone
yak your life away
no promise to betray
gone gone gone
somebody else will pay
the national debt no way
gone gone gone
your furniture layaway

plan gone astray
gone gone gone
made hay
gone gone gone
Sunk in Baiae's Bay
yes it's gone gone gone
wallet and all you say
gone gone gone
so you can waive your pay
yes it's gone gone gone
gone last Saturday
yes it's gone gone gone
tomorrow's another day
gone gone gone
bald & old & gay
gone gone gone
turned old and gray
yes it's gone gone gone
whitebeard & cold
yes it's gone gone gone
cashmere scarf & gold
yes it's gone gone gone
warp & woof & wold
yes it's gone gone gone
gone far far away
to the home of the brave
down into the grave
yes it's gone gone gone
moon beneath the wave
yes it's gone gone gone
so I end this song
yes this song is gone
gone to kick the gong
yes it's gone gone gone
No more right & wrong
yes it's gone gone gone
gone gone away

November 10, 1996

Reverse the rain of Terror . . .

Reverse the rain of Terror on street consciousness U.S.A.
Death Penalty! Electric Chair! A roomsful of poison gas! Lethal
        injections! Mortal Hanging! Beheading the Idiot killer!
Dogs slaver over airport luggage! Suitcase bottoms caked with hash!
        Strip search the sick opium addict, medicine's up his anus in
        a finger stall
arriving from legal India, cozy England, lax Morocco, face 12 billion
        Dollars worth of cops
Sniffing bodies for illegal medicine! Vomiting in a stone cell,
        abdominal convulsions, muscle spasms thigh & foot, sleepless
        cold-turkey torture—
Puerto Rican kid needs a doctor, young black man needs his girlfriend's
        fix, white boy didn't know his habit was immortal!
The octogenarian schmecker's liver & kidneys failed, wants a
        deathbed shot of M
Half mad lady on the street had a fight with her daughter the whore!
The old boy lies on the sidewalk hands dirty red faced in his own
        saliva.
The delicate youth's in his halfway house a decade, thorazine eyes
        glazed over
His brother's Christmas card arrives at Binghampton State Hospital!
The elder hides in a furnished room drinks wine delivers newspapers,
        didn't wanna work on the neutron bomb!
The salesman's product went off the market, recycling coke bottles he
        cries at kitchen tables blaming Jews
An auto worker shoveling snow curses six African-Americans mugged
        him twenty years ago—
A black man walked the street with his B.A. pager, clubbed down
        giving lip to a cop car
The young fruit dies body with sores he challenged the Senate on the
        plague.
The homeless jewish guitarist sings on the 14th Street's L Train
        Subway platform, blows harmonica, taps tambourine with one
        foot, with another drums

then back to his graybeard cocksucker's apartment fries eggs
Streetcorner boys and girlfriends hang round the butcher shop
      corner, "Smoke smoke?"
Rocky Flats engineers tear their hair, Plutonium waste'll outlast an
      otherworldly God

December 1996

Sending Message

They are sending a message to the youth of America
Smoking medical marijuana's all right
They're sending a message in cartoon saloons hard-ass blokes look
       like camels smoke Camels at the bar, 5 year olds love it,
To the youth of America they're sending a message
CIA no official connections to Contra coke dealers in *New York Times*
Washington Post expert crackheads send same messages to adoles-
       cent Senior citizen crackhead readers
They're sending a message to American youth, African youth can
       starve to death we can't care
too much money, far over the Atlantic, our boys'll never die, politi-
       cally unpopular, they'll become dependent, it won't fly
They're sending message by Bronco, Honda, 4 by 4, cinema MG, Land
       Rover & half million gas stations
youth of this nation fossil fuel's neat, hella cool, admirable dope really
       rad, as if—what valley girls think when their fathers drive
       them to Highschool—
They're sending the message to Saturn, American Democracy works
       over the globe, spin that round your rings
To Chinese youth, eat like us, we do flesh & fries,
Don't sleep on streets, dangerous off-duty death-squad police send
       this message to Brazilian kiddies
Someone sent naked pretty boys on FCC Internet, Don't!
No Forbidden Planet Swedish sex? Got the message pretty girls?
Got the message clean old men? Michelangelo got the message? Da
       Vinci got it? Phidias, Socrates, Shakespeare, J. Edgar Hoover
       at the Plaza, Cardinal Francis Spellman on Roy Cohn's yacht,
       Senator Jesse Helms in your gut, duh
got the message teeny-weenies? They're sending a message right
       below your belly button.
A message to the youth of America, "Diminished expectations," they's
       too many people,
native gooks work cheaper, rich get richer, North hemispheric whites
       live longer, Black high-blood pressure rules Kentucky Fried
       Chicken

Across the highway from Arbie's Barbecue Palace, Roy Rogers' Horse-
        chops, or McDonalds Amazon Treeburgers
you heard about on Television serves the message Eat your meat
or beat your meat, safe sex with ketchup, Whatever
The message now's pay 4 trillion dollars debt Reagan pissed away on
        Military,
promised before you born, sit in school waterclosets study yr Latin
They're sending youth a message look at TV football baseball hypnotic
        soccer basketball sports, sport!
General Rios-Montt & Pat Robertson sent a message to Guatemalan
        Indians
so 200,000 dropped dead with delight at sight of Christ's military
pistol machete machinegun baseball bat & Inerrant Bible
700 Club's Antichrist sends U.S. youth this message Despise the poor
        & piss on liberal Jesus
The message is Compassion'll cause a Wall Street crash
& Networks send me messages Shut the fuck up.

December 3, 1996, 4:30 A.M.
New York City

No! No! It's Not the End

No! No!
    Not the end of
        Civilization
    Not the end of
        Civilization

Blast of industrial
    Gas in Bhopal
        No! No! Not the end of
        Civilization

Dropt one bomb
    killed one
        hundred thousand
    Hiroshima nineteen forty five

No no not the end of
        Civilization
    Not the end of Civilization

Guatemala murdered
    two hundred thousand
        Indians

No no not the end of
        Civilization
    Not the end of Civilization

200 thousand
    slaughtered in Rwanda
    Crazed events
        on the TV screen

No no not the end of
                Civilization
        Not the end of Civilization

U.S. Blacks in jail
                land of the free
        mosta these citizens you & me

No no not the end of
                Civilization
        Not the end of Civilization

Fossil fuel dust filling heaven
        ozone layer hole in the sky

No no not the end of
                Civilization
        Not the end of Civilization

Oldest trees in the world cut down
        Weyerhaeuser Bush wears a cardboard Crown

No no not the end of
                Civilization
        Not the end of Civilization

Amazon forests cut to the ground
        you can still breathe
                to the chainsaw's sound

No no not the end of
                Civilization
        Only a temporary aberration

No No it's not the end of Civilization
It's Nobadaddy's
        old temptation
No no it's not the end of Civilization
Everybody's waltzing
        to "the Hesitation"

It's the same damned
President's Inauguration
No no it's not the end of Civilization
We're come to "the fabled
damned of Nations"
No no it's not the end of Civilization
Slaves wore chains
at the States' creation
No no it's not the end of Civilization
sourpuss wantsa stop colored immigration
Nobody's wearing
hooves & scales
all they wanna do is
kill more whales
No no it's not the end of Civilization

No no it's not the end of Civilization
Cayenne saved a little bit of sensation
No no it's not the end of civilization
No final solution
just gas & cremation

December 18–20, 1996

Bad Poem

Being as Now has been re-invented
I have devised a new now
Entering the real Now
at last
which is now

December 24, 1996, 3 A.M.

Homeless Compleynt

Pardon me buddy, I didn't mean to bug you
      but I came from Vietnam
where I killed a lot of Vietnamese gentlemen
          a few ladies too
and I couldn't stand the pain
          and got a habit out of fear
& I've gone through rehab and I'm clean
      but I got no place to sleep
            and I don't know what to do
            with myself right now

I'm sorry buddy, I didn't mean to bug you
      but it's cold in the alley
          & my heart's sick alone
and I'm clean, but my life's a mess
      Third Avenue
          and E. Houston Street
on the corner traffic island under a red light
wiping your windshield with a dirty rag

December 24, 1996

Happy New Year Robert & June

Happy New Year Robert & June
Tho I'd hoped to see you soon
I'd better say Happy Hanukkah too
Till I get your number that's new—
I'll be leaving for retreat,
Where they make me salt-free meat
along with Gelek Rinpoche
Who's got ailments same as me,
in Michigan Camp Copneconic
Where I'll room with Mr. Harmonic
Philip Glass in our Buddhist Class
Ten days later January 8
I'll go to Boston, rest & wait
the weekend in anticipation
Maybe a hernia operation
supervised by Dr. Lown
(cardiologist of wide renown
—I'd recommended him to you
elderly trustworthy smart & true)
—Recuperate a week with Ellie
Dorfman, eat yellow fish-yuckh jelly
with Gefilte fish, then best
Mid January home NY to rest
Maybe we'll see eachother then,
in any case let me know when.

Love, Allen
December 12, 1996

Diamond Bells

"Clear light & illusion body become one"

Hearing the all pervading scintillation of empty bells I realize
Napoleon had toes
Frankenstein's big toe
Hayagriva cosmic horse one big cleft toe
Virgin Mary white-toed married Joseph brown-toed, impregnated by
        a white dove transparent triple-toed
How many toes has God? Yahweh nobody knows his toes
Allah's toes? Mohammed, prophetic ten
Jesus Christ well-kissed human toes
Sealo the Seal Boy who two-fingered hand-flippers at shoulders could
        smoke & type with regular ten toes
sold tiny white toilets wrapped in toilet paper, souvenirs one dollar
Shelly ten pale pure toes
Michelangelo enjoyed five digits per foot, Da Vinci mapped ten on his
        two feet
Flies toes get stuck on spiderwebs
Spiders slide swift-toed on sticky nets
Scratch the sole, toes curl
Foetus is capable of toes
Stubbed my bare fourth toe on a step ladder one dark Friday night,
        though it still wiggles
walking on snowy mud's painful, back aches
John Madison has chocolate toes
Hitler natural toes
Buddha ten bare toes enlightened
Lay my skull on night pillows, rest on Tara's lap between gentle toes
Lama YabYum dreams with 20 toes
Emptiness innumerable trillion toes
Old men's toenails thicken ivory aged
Dead toenails grow in cenotaphs
Napoleon wore toenails inside polished riding boots
Elephant toenail stubs nudge tussocks
Such is the all pervading scintillation of empty bells

December 30, 1996, 12:55 A.M.

Virtual Impunity Blues

With Virtual impunity Clinton got campaign funds from pink Chinese
With Virtual impunity CIA Contra stringers sold Cocaine disease L.A.
        & Minneapolis
With Virtual impunity FBI burned down apocalyptic Waco
With Virtual impunity gov't began charging huge fees for public
        college studies
With Virtual impunity Congress FCC ok'd Fundamentalist Broadcast
        censorship
With Virtual impunity Family Values insulted ladies, gays, Afric
        Americans
With Virtual impunity the Pope banned planet birth control
With Virtual impunity N. Carolina banned sodomy in the wrong hole
With Virtual impunity the Chinese banned fresh speech electrics
With Virtual impunity Albanian Lottery bosses bought & sold elections

January 1997

Waribashi

Walk into your local Japanese restaurant Teriyaki Boy—
order sliced raw fish mackerel, smoked eel, roe on vinagered rice balls
slide thin wooden utensils out a white paper sleeve with blue Crane print
split the wood, rub ends together smooth down splinters, sit & wait & sigh—
200,000 cubic meters Southeast Asian timber exports
sawed & processed in Japan, resold, 20 billion waribashi
used once, thrown away—roots of rainforest destruction—help pay interest
Thailand's & Malaysia's yearly debt service to World Bank, IMF—
Your plate arrives with sharp green mustard & pink pickled ginger slices
new sprig of parsley, lift the chopsticks to your mouth enjoy sashimi

January 7, 1997, 6:30 A.M.

Good Luck

I'm lucky to have all five fingers on the right hand
Lucky peepee with little pain
Lucky bowels move
Lucky, sleep nights on a captain's bed, nap mid-afternoons
Lucky to amble down First Avenue
Lucky make a couple hundred thousand a year
singing Eli Eli, writing passing mind, etching primordial doodles,
       teaching Buddhist college, snapping Leica bus-stop photos
       thru my window eyeballs
Hear ambulance sirens, smell garlic & rust, taste persimmons &
       flounder, walk the loft floor barefoot soles a little desensitized
Lucky I can think, and sky can snow

January 8, 1997

Some Little Boys Dont

Some little boys like it
Some little boys dont
Some little girls swipe it
Some little girls won't

Some nephews suck it
Some lollypops grunt
Some nieces truck it
If grandpa's a runt

Some puberties request it
Four times a month
Some girl teens breast it
Some eat it for brunch

Some little people gargle
Some adolescents warble
Some teenyboppers babble
Some kiddies play Scrabble

January 10, 1997, 4 A.M.

Jacking Off

Who showed up?
      Joe S. pale bodied wiry leanness,
      suck your cock—I kissed his belly,
      thin muscular breast—
Suck my cock you bitch, little bitch
      suck my cock,
Huck, I got him on his knees
      licked his ass his hairy behind
      doggie style, jacked him off he
      grabbed his own dick finished—come.
Tom G. big cocked passed thru my
      dream bed, didn't stay
Ah John got you, bought the
      leather handcuffs & strap
      binding hand & feet helpless,
      Leather collar roped to the
      bedstead's head—buy it
      once for all S&M shops
      Christopher Street
      Uptown leather
Spank good & hard, slap his ass
      let him writhe, better
      than cutting him up,
      designs with razor—
So came on that unfamiliar fear
      savage control over
      Adonis body, willing
      eager—bound to be true.

January 28, 1997

Think Tank Rhymes

think tank
pick thank
lamb shank
wet wank
drug dork
hankie pankey
kitchey camp
namby pamby
macho wimp
witchy granny
randy daddy
skimpy mammie
toilet Tilly
itchy nursie
Golden Grammie
dandy Sammy

Fried pork
mind wonk
brain konk
junk funk
coke dink
dead drunk
Big Pink
skunk stink
mom wink
nuke kink
big dick
instinct
gum crank
space pork
fried wok

Hershey drink
Einstein

January 30, 1997, 2:45 A.M.

Song of the Washing Machine

Burned out Burned out Burned out
We're not burned out We're not burned out
for a house for a house for a house for a house
Bathroom Bathroom Bathroom Bathroom
At home at home at home at home
We're not burned out We're not burned out
Fair enough fair enough fair enough
Can you account for yourself account for yourself
Better not better not better not better not

January 31, 1997

World Bank Blues

I work for the world bank yes I do
My salary was hundred thousand smackeroo
I know my Harvard economics better than you

Nobody knows that I make big plans
I show Madagascar leaders how to dance
How to read statistics & wear striped pants

Emotional statistics that's not my job
Facts & figures, I'm no slob
But foresting & farming's all a big blob

Here's our scheme to stabilize your paper
for International trade right now or later
Follow our advice you'll thank your creator

Whatcha got to export, what raw materials?
Monoculture diamonds, coffee, Cereals
Sell 'em on the market to Multinational Imperials

We'll loan you money to expand production
Pay our yearly interest, for your own protection
Tighten your belts, we'll have no objection

Throw in some little minimal principle
tho debt service paid makes the deal invincible
That takes dollars but your currency's exchangeable

Get people working on mass market land
cut down forests, for your cash in hand
Or superhighways money where Rainforests stand

With agribusiness farms you can export beef
Cut social services & poverty relief
Forest people shift to the cities in grief

Tighten your belt for a roller coaster ride
Production's up, market prices slide
Wood pulp burger meat, coffee downside

Increase production pay yr. World Bank debt—
At least the interest if that's all you can get
Cut down Amazon you haven't paid it yet

In one decade you give all the money back
As Bank debt service but the Principal, alack!
We'll lend more cash (but dont sell smack)

Austerity measures, wages go down,
th'urban sewage is a charnel ground
Buses fall apart at the edge of town

coral reef fish dead factory waste,
Indigines hooked on Yankee dollar taste
Swiss bank funds for dictators disgraced

Fauna killed for the debt Costa Rica
Unknown flora at the mouth of Boca Chica
Birds in Equador, sick with toxic leakage?

Riots start over bags of foreign rice
Arm your teenage army with U.S. mace
Borrow money for a local Arms race

Families driven from crop land to forests
Forest folk in hovels hid from tourists
Currencies bankrupt for free market purists?

I just retired from my 20 year job
at World Bank Central with the money mob
Go to AA meetings so's not die a slob

I worked in Africa, Americas, Vietnam
Bangkok too with World Banks' big clan
Now I'm retired and I don't give a damn

Walk the streets of Washington alone at night
The job I did, was it wrong was it right?
Big mistakes that've gone out of sight?

It wasn't the job of a bureaucrat like me
to check the impact of the Bank policy
When debt bore fruit on the world money tree.

February 1997

Richard III

Toenail-thickening age on me,
Sugar coating my nerves, leg
   muscles lacking blood, weak kneed
Heart insufficient, a thick'd valve-wall,
Short of breath, six pounds
   overweight with water—
logged liver, gut & lung— up at 4 a.m.
   reading Shakespeare.

         February 4, 1997, 4:03 A.M., NYC

Death & Fame

When I die
I don't care what happens to my body
throw ashes in the air, scatter 'em in East River
bury an urn in Elizabeth New Jersey, B'nai Israel Cemetery
But I want a big funeral
St. Patrick's Cathedral, St. Mark's Church, the largest synagogue in
       Manhattan
First, there's family, brother, nephews, spry aged Edith stepmother
       96, Aunt Honey from old Newark,
Doctor Joel, cousin Mindy, brother Gene one eyed one ear'd, sister-
       in-law blonde Connie, five nephews, stepbrothers & sisters
       their grandchildren,
companion Peter Orlovsky, caretakers Rosenthal & Hale, Bill Morgan—
Next, teacher Trungpa Vajracharya's ghost mind, Gelek Rinpoche
       there, Sakyong Mipham, Dalai Lama alert, chance visiting
       America, Satchitananda Swami,
Shivananda, Dehorahava Baba, Karmapa XVI, Dudjom Rinpoche,
       Katagiri & Suzuki Roshi's phantoms
Baker, Whalen, Daido Loori, Qwong, Frail White-haired Kapleau
       Roshis, Lama Tarchin—
Then, most important, lovers over half-century
Dozens, a hundred, more, older fellows bald & rich
young boys met naked recently in bed, crowds surprised to see each
       other, innumerable, intimate, exchanging memories
"He taught me to meditate, now I'm an old veteran of the thousand
       day retreat—"
"I played music on subway platforms, I'm straight but loved him he
       loved me"
"I felt more love from him at 19 than ever from anyone"
"We'd lie under covers gossip, read my poetry, hug & kiss belly to belly
       arms round each other"
"I'd always get into his bed with underwear on & by morning my
       skivvies would be on the floor"
"Japanese, always wanted take it up my bum with a master"

"We'd talk all night about Kerouac & Cassady sit Buddhalike then
	sleep in his captain's bed."
"He seemed to need so much affection, a shame not to make him happy"
"I was lonely never in bed nude with anyone before, he was so gentle my
	stomach
shuddered when he traced his finger along my abdomen nipple to hips—"
"All I did was lay back eyes closed, he'd bring me to come with mouth
	& fingers along my waist"
"He gave great head"
So there be gossip from loves of 1946, ghost of Neal Cassady commin-
	gling with flesh and youthful blood of 1997
and surprise—"You too? But I thought you were straight!"
"I am but Ginsberg an exception, for some reason he pleased me,"
"I forgot whether I was straight gay queer or funny, was myself, tender
	and affectionate to be kissed on the top of my head,
my forehead throat heart & solar plexus, mid-belly, on my prick,
	tickled with his tongue my behind"
"I loved the way he'd recite 'But at my back always hear/ time's winged
	chariot hurrying near,' heads together, eye to eye, on a
	pillow—"
Among lovers one handsome youth straggling the rear
"I studied his poetry class, 17 year-old kid, ran some errands to his
	walk-up flat,
seduced me didn't want to, made me come, went home, never saw him
	again never wanted to . . ."
"He couldn't get it up but loved me," "A clean old man," "He made
	sure I came first"
This the crowd most surprised proud at ceremonial place of honor—
Then poets & musicians—college boys' grunge bands—age-old rock
	star Beatles, faithful guitar accompanists, gay classical con-
	ductors, unknown high Jazz music composers, funky trum-
	peters, bowed bass & french horn black geniuses, folksinger
	fiddlers with dobro tambourine harmonica mandolin auto-
	harp pennywhistles & kazoos
Next, artist Italian romantic realists schooled in mystic 60's India,
	late fauve Tuscan painter-poets, Classic draftsman Massa-
	chusetts surreal jackanapes with continental wives, poverty
	sketchbook gesso oil watercolor masters from American
	provinces

Then highschool teachers, lonely Irish librarians, delicate biblio-
          philes, sex liberation troops nay armies, ladies of either sex
"I met him dozens of times he never remembered my name I loved
          him anyway, true artist"
"Nervous breakdown after menopause, his poetry humor saved me
          from suicide hospitals"
"Charmant, genius with modest manners, washed sink dishes, my
          studio guest a week in Budapest"
Thousands of readers, "Howl changed my life in Libertyville Illinois"
"I saw him read Montclair State Teachers College decided be a poet— "
"He turned me on, I started with garage rock sang my songs in Kansas
          City"
"Kaddish made me weep for myself & father alive in Nevada City"
"Father Death comforted me when my sister died Boston 1982"
"I read what he said in a newsmagazine, blew my mind, realized
          others like me out there"
Deaf & Dumb bards with hand signing quick brilliant gestures
Then Journalists, editors' secretaries, agents, portraitists & photo-
          graphy aficionados, rock critics, cultured laborors, cultural
          historians come to witness the historic funeral
Super-fans, poetasters, aging Beatniks & Deadheads, autograph-
          hunters, distinguished paparazzi, intelligent gawkers
Everyone knew they were part of "History" except the deceased
who never knew exactly what was happening even when I was alive

                                             February 22, 1997

Sexual Abuse

"A Nation of Finks"
—*W. S. Burroughs*

A voice in the kitchen light:
Sexual abuse should not be
      rewarded with a wink
Sexshual abuse should not be
      revarded mit a vink
Re Boston-Herald headline "Sexual Abuse Law Targets Clergy"
"Senator: Religious leaders must report child molesters"
Priests should turn each other in, fink—
So, say it in the confession box, not
      over sherry at intimate dinner.

February 26, 1997, 6 A.M.

Butterfly Mind

The mind is like a butterfly
That lights upon a rose
or flutters to a stinky feces pile
swoops into smoky bus exhaust
or rests upon porch chair, a flower breathing
open & closed balancing a Tennessee breeze—
Flies to Texas for a convention
spring weeds in fields of oil rigs
Some say these rainbow wings have soul
Some say empty brain
tiny automatic large-eyed wings
that settle on the page.

January 29, 1997, 2:15 A.M., NYC

A fellow named Steven

A fellow named Steven
went to look for God
on a street that's even
and a street that's odd

A lifestyle clean
with music and wife
A golden mean
For a heavenly life

He went to the city
Tried all tricks
Sadness & pity
many highs, many kicks

Saved by music
Books & dance bands,
Generous, correct
Taught class, steady hands

Married, had a boy
Whom he sang into life
He'll long enjoy
His Child & Wife

Air Shuttle Boston–N.Y.
March 4, 1997, 5 P.M. in milky sky

Half Asleep

Moved six months ago left it behind for Peter
He'd been in Almora when we bought it,
an old blanket, brown Himalayan wool
two-foot-wide long strips of light cloth
bound together with wool strings
That after 3 decades began to loosen
Soft familiar with use in Benares & Manhattan
I took it in my hands, searched to match the seams,
       fold them, sew together as I thought
But myself, being ill, too heavy for my arms,
Leave it to housekeeper's repair
       it disappeared suddenly in my hands—
back to the old apartment
where I'd let go half year before

March 7, 1997

Objective Subject

It's true I write about myself
Who else do I know so well?
Where else gather blood red roses & kitchen garbage
What else has my thick heart, hepatitis or hemorrhoids—
Who else lived my seventy years, my old Naomi?
and if by chance I scribe U.S. politics, Wisdom
meditation, theories of art
it's because I read a newspaper loved
teachers skimmed books or visited a museum

March 8, 1997, 12:30 A.M.

Kerouac

I can't answer,
reason I can't answer
I haven't been dead yet
Don't remember dead
I'm on 14th St & 1st Avenue
Vat's the qvestion?

March 12, 1997

Hepatitis Body Itch . . .

Hepatitis
Body itch
nausea
hemorrhage
tender Hemorrhoids
High Blood
Sugar, low
leaden limbs
lassitude
bed rest
shit factory
this corpse
cancer

March 13, 1997

Whitmanic Poem

We children, we
        school boys,
girls in America
        laborers, students
dominated by lust

March 18, 1997

American Sentences 1995–1997

I felt a breeze below my waist and realized that my fly was open.

April 20, 1995

*   *   *

Sitting forward elbows on knees, oh what luck! to be able to crap!

April 17, 1995

"That was good! that was great! That was important!" Standing to flush the toilet.

June 22, 1995

Relief! relief! O Boy O Boy! That was necessary, wash behind!

January 18, 1997

"A good shit is worth a thousand dollars if your purse can afford it."

February 10, 1997, 5 A.M.

Heard at every workplace—obnoxious slogan: "Shit or get off the pot!"

January 24, 1997

How did I know? How did my ass know? Suddenly, go to the bathroom!

March 10, 1997

*   *   *

Château d'Amboise

Sun setting on their faces the diners chatter over plates of duck.

June 22, 1995

Baul Song

"Oh my mad mind, my mad mind, where've you been all my life, my old
mad mind?"

October 7, 1996

The three-day-old kitchen fly's flown into my bedroom for company.

December 9, 1996

"Hi-diddly-Dee, a poet's life for me," Gregory Corso sang in Paris
sniffing H.

January 16, 1997

Chopping apples for the fruit compote—suffer, suffer, suffer, suffer!

January 24, 1997

Courageous little lemon with so many pits! sliced into the pot.

January 25, 1997

The young dog—he jumped out the TV tube stood still then barked for
supper.

January 26, 1997

Stupid of me, stupid of me, just dumb plain stupid ass! Where's my
pen?

February 19, 1997, 2:45 A.M.

My father dying of Cancer, head drooping, "Oy kindelach."

February 24, 1997

Whatcha do about little girls who want to play Horsey on my knee?

March 10, 1997

"Hey Buster! Whatcha looking at me like that for?" in the Bronx
subway.

March 10, 1997, 2:45 A.M.

To see Void vast infinite look out the window into the blue sky.

March 23, 1997

Variations on Ma Rainey's See See Rider

"I've been down at the bus stop
    Buy my jellyroll there
If I can't sell it in Memphis
        you can
    buy it in Eau St. Claire.
See See Rider
      you got me
           in your chair
     But if I have
        my fanny
           can sell it anywhere
     See what I want today
         yes yes yes
     Need a man who
        really can do
anything I say
     Do that for me
        Then I
          guess I
    won't go way.

Go way go way go way from here
    look for all old gray home
    I can live by myself and
      ring my telephone
    Dirty pictures on my new TV
      Just now turned them on
    I don't need you and your
        mamma's long time gone

March 3, 1997

Sky Words

Sunrise dazzles the eye
Sirens echo tear thru the sky
Taxi klaxons echo the street
Broken car horns bleat bleat bleat

Sky is covered with words
Day is covered with words
Night is covered with words
God is covered with words

Consciousness covered with words
Mind is covered with words
Life & Death are words
Words are covered with words

Lovers are covered with words
Murders are covered with words
Spies are covered with words
Governments covered with words

Mustard gas covered with words
Hydrogen Bombs covered with words
World "News" is words
Wars are covered with words

Secret police covered with words
Starvation covered with words
Mothers bones covered with words
Skeleton Children made of words

Armies are covered with words
Money covered with words
High Finance covered with words
Poverty Jungles covered with words

Electric chairs covered with words
Screaming crowds are covered with words
Tyrant radios covered with words
Hell's televised, covered with words

March 23, 1997, 5 A.M.

Scatalogical Observations

The Ass knows more than the mind knows

Young romantic readers
Skip this part of the book
If you want a glimpse of life
You're free to take a look

Shit machine shit machine
I'm an incredible shit machine
Piss machine Piss machine
Inexhaustible piss machine

Piss & shit machine
That's the Golden Mean
Whether young or old
Move your bowels of gold

Piss & shit machine
It always comes out clean
Whether you're old or young
Never hold your tongue

(Chorus)
Shit machine piss machine
I'm an incredible piss machine
Piss machine piss machine
Inexhaustible shit machine.

Brown or black or green
everything will be seen
Hard or soft or loose
Shit's a glimpse of Truth

Babe or boy or youth
Fart's without a tooth
Baby girl or maid
Many a fart in laid

Shit piss shit piss
Fuck & shit & piss
Fuck fart shit Piss
It all comes down to this

Beautiful male Madonnas
Wrathful Maids of Honor
To be frank & honest
Stink the watercloset

Shit machine piss machine
Much comes down to this
Piss machine shit machine
Nature's not obscene

Shit piss shit piss
How'll I end my song?
Shit piss shit piss
Nature never wrong

(Chorus)
Shit machine Piss Machine
I'm an incredible piss machine
Piss machine shit machine
Inexhaustible shit machine

March 23, 1997

My Team Is Red Hot

My dick is red hot
Your dick is diddly dot

My politics red hot
Your politics diddly-plot

My President's red hot
your President's diddly-blot

My land is red hot
Your land is diddly-knot

My nation's red hot
Your nation's diddly rot

My cosmos red hot
Your cosmos diddly iddly squat

March 23, 1997

Starry Rhymes

Sun rises east
Sun sets west
Nobody knows
What the sun knows best

North star north
Southern Cross south
Hold close the universe
In your mouth

Gemini high
Pleiades low
Winter sky
Begins to snow

Orion down
North Star up
Fiery leaves
Begin to drop

March 23, 1997, 4:51 A.M.

Thirty State Bummers

Take a pee pee take a Bum
Take your choice for number one

Old man more or someone new
Take your choice someone new

President Clinton President Dole
Number three you're in a hole

Anchor two or anchor four
One's a liar one's a bore

Richard Helms Angleton live
We were lucky to survive

Jesse Helms & dirty pix
Dance your fate with his party mix

Idi Amin General Mobutu
Were paid by me & you

They were bought by me & mine
Albania, number 9

Mr. Allende was number 10
Pinochet Dictator then

Death squads in El Salvador
We paid D'Aubisson to score

Guatamalas by the dozen
Pat Robertson was country cousin

Rios-Montt the Indian killer
Born-again General Bible pillar

Nicaragua squeezed between
Col. North & a cocaine queen

Drug Czar Bush gave Company moolah
To Noriega Panama's ruler

Venezuela's Drug War Chief
Turned around to be a thief

Mexico's general drug-war head
pumped informers full of lead

State Department's favorite bloke
In Haiti he sold tons of coke

Till Aristide unhex'd the curse
CIA filled Cedras' Purse

White Peru's its Indian shame
Gave "Shining Path" worldwide fame

Then dictator Fujimori
Paid the World Bank hunky dory

With Indian Class the majority
Peru got respectable with poverty

Made a deal with English banks
To pay back USA with thanks

The price of rubber tin went down
Cocaine syndicates come to town

Now the money's in cocaine crops
U.S. Hellies do their dope air drops

We got rid of the President of Costa Rica
He had no army he didn't kill people

Lots began in '53
Guatemala couldn't break free

United Fruits annulled the vote
As Alan & Foster Dulles gloat

Then unseated Mosaddeq
& left Iran a police-state wreck

Then we sold the guy in Iraq
Money to bomb Iranians back

Central America Middle East
Preyed on by "Great Satan's" beast

Worst of all, & hell be damned!
Think what happened in Vietnam

Laos, victim of the war
Nobody really knew what for

Cambodia, caught by the tail
When we blew up Mekong's Ho Chi Minh Trail,

Descended into Anarchy
Pol Pot's Maoist Butchery

Shihanook's book before that day
Was called "My War with the CIA"

Who's to blame, Who's to blame
Anybody share America's shame

But there's more! Count the score!
So far we got twenty-four

25 is Afghanistan
Fundamentalists armed by The Man

Tribal Drug Lord Mountain gangs
Veiling up their own sex thangs

Looking around for number 26
Indochina was the Colonial sticks

France introduced the opium crop
France would sell the Chinese hop

Britain, U.S. got in on the deal
Opium war made the Emperor kneel

China opened to our own junk men
Shanghai famous for the opium den

Strung out on junk we took their silk
The yellow peril drank Christian milk

We're doing exactly the same thing again
In Indochina with Marlboro men

Smoke our dope to be Favored Nation
Nicotine cancer next generation

Who's pushing this new dope ring?
Senator Jesse Helms the Moralist King

Peaches Prunes & company goons
For the next two-hundred eighty eight moons

NAFTA NAFTA what comes after?
Toxic waste—Industrial laughter

Industrial Smog, Industrial sneers
Industrial women weeping tears

Wages low no CIO
No medical plan oh no! no! no!

No FDR No WPA
No toilet time, human say

No overtime no other way
Yankee work for a dollar a day

No jobs today No jobless pay
No future life but turn to clay

Work hard for a little bit of honey
But USA takes all the money

March 24, 1997, 10:40 P.M.

I have a nosebleed You have a nosebleed
He has a nosebleed three
She has a nosebleed It has a nosebleed
They all bleed on me

March 24, 1997

Timmy made a hot milk
Better than a warm milk
Better than a cold milk shake
Hot cream warm cream oh La La!
Pretty boy straight kids, Ha ha ha
Sneakers Jeans & T-shirts, damn!
Got it made said houseboy Sam
All except the Ku Klux Klan
Wham Bam & thank you ma'm

March 25, 1997, 6:30 A.M.

This kind of Hepatitis can cause ya
Nosebleed skin itch bowel nausea
Swell up hanging hemorrhoid heads
Easter lilies by your hospital beds

March 24, 1997

Giddy-yup giddy-yup giddy-yap
I can't take more of your crap
Giddy-yap Giddy-yap Giddy-yup
So you're right, so you're right, Shut up!
Giddy yup shut up, Giddy yup shut up
Giddy-yap giddy yap giddy yap shut up.

March 24, 1997

Turn on the heat & take a seat
& lookit junkies on the street

Forget the news from old Time-Warner
Lookit crackheads on the corner

Turn off TV 7 o'clock
They're selling grass around the block

Minimum wage is whacha make
Narcs are mostly on the take.

Make big money from your mob
Till Old MacDonald makes a job.

March 25, 1997

Bop Sh'bam

OO Bop Sh'bam
At the poetry slam
Scream & yell
At the poetry ball

Get in a rage
On the poetry stage
Make it rhyme
In double-time

Talk real fast
till your time's passed
Sound like a clown
& then sit down.

Listen to the next
'cause she listened to you
Tho all she says is
Peek-a-boo-boo.

March 25, 1997, 3:30 P.M.

Dream

There was a bulge in my right side, this dream recently—just now I realized I had a baby, full grown that came out of my right abdomen while I in hospital with dangerous hepatitis C.

I lay there awhile, wondering what to do, half grateful, half apprehensive. It'll need milk, it'll need exercise, taken out into fresh air with baby carriage.

Peter there sympathetic, he'll help me, bent over my bed, kissed me, happy a child to care for. What compassion he has. Reassured I felt the miracle was in Peter's reliable hands—but gee what if he began drinking again? No this'll keep him straight. How care for a baby, what can I do?

Worried & pleased since it was true I slowly woke, still thinking it'd happened, consciousness returned slowly 2:29 AM I was awake and there's no little mystic baby—naturally appeared, just disappeared—

A glow of happiness next morn, warm glow of pleasure half the day.

March 27, 1997, 4 A.M.

Things I'll Not Do (Nostalgias)

Never go to Bulgaria, had a booklet & invitation
Same Albania, invited last year, privately by Lottery scammers or
      recovering alcoholics,
Or enlightened poets of the antique land of Hades Gates
Nor visit Lhasa live in Hilton or Ngawang Gelek's household & weary
      ascend Potala
Nor ever return to Kashi "oldest continuously habited city in world"
      bathe in Ganges & sit again at Manikarnika ghat with Peter,
      visit Lord Jagganath again in Puri, never back to Birbhum take
      notes tales of Khaki Baba
Or hear music festivals in Madras with Philip
Or return to have Chai with older Sunil & the young coffeeshop poets,
Tie my head on a block in the Chinatown opium den, pass by Moslem
      Hotel, its rooftop Tinsmith Street Choudui Chowh Nimtallah
      Burning ground nor smoke ganja on the Hooghly
Nor the alleyways of Achmed's Fez, nevermore drink mint tea at Soco
      Chico, visit Paul B. in Tangiers
Or see the Sphinx in Desert at Sunrise or sunset, morn & dusk in the
      desert
Ancient collapsed Beirut, sad bombed Babylon & Ur of old, Syria's
      grim mysteries all Araby & Saudi Deserts, Yemen's sprightly
      folk,
Old opium tribal Afghanistan, Tibet-Templed Beluchistan
See Shanghai again, nor cares of Dunhuang
Nor climb E. 12th Street's stairway 3 flights again,
Nor go to literary Argentina, accompany Glass to Sao Paolo & live a
      month in a flat Rio's beaches & favella boys, Bahia's great
      Carnival
Nor more daydream of Bali, too far Adelaide's festival to get new song
      sticks
Not see the new slums of Jakarta, mysterious Borneo forests & painted
      men & women
No more Sunset Boulevard, Melrose Avenue, Oz on Ocean Way
Old cousin Danny Leegant, memories of Aunt Edith in Santa Monica

No more sweet summers with lovers, teaching Blake at Naropa,
Mind Writing Slogans, new modern American Poetics, Williams
       Kerouac Reznikoff Rakosi Corso Creeley Orlovsky
Any visits to B'nai Israel graves of Buba, Aunt Rose, Harry Meltzer and
       Aunt Clara, Father Louis
Not myself except in an urn of ashes

March 30, 1997, A.M.

AFTERWORD
On Death & Fame

This final collection of Allen Ginsberg poems completes a remarkable half century of continuous verse creation. Allen leaves nothing out and takes the readers down a final walk of sickness and decline, but still the illumination of life shines through these strophes and rhythms. In these final five years, Allen struggles through several transformations. He is placed under the ever intensifying glare of media attention as a founder of the Beat Generation. He is interviewed as a living icon/prophet to each generation from the 1940s through the 1990s and is expected to elucidate the meaning of the century's conclusion and make new millennial predictions. The telephones ring continually for talk and advice on every subject from presidential politics to baby naming. He finally manages to place his lifelong archives into a permanent home at Stanford University. He is reviled in the *New York Times* on several occasions for "selling out." For the first time in his life, he buys himself a bit of comfort. At age seventy, he leaves his fourth-floor walk-up tenement apartment and moves into an elevator loft building still within his beloved Lower East Side of Manhattan. In these years, he embraces Jewel Heart Buddhist Center in Ann Arbor, Michigan, where he attends retreats, performs benefits, and receives profound and ultimate instructions from his teacher Gelek Rinpoche. Although struggling with illnesses continually, he does not learn of his fatal diagnosis until a week before his last breath. The poems follow these paths and illumine our own lives.

"New Democracy Wish List" was written at the request of *Long Island Newsday*. Allen polled his friends and collected advice on various subjects. The poem was sent to the White House and politely received. Allen's diabetes led to a state of dysesthesia below the waist. Allen transformed any shame of incontinence to a celebration of aging and life, as in "Here We Go 'Round the Mulberry Bush." It was Allen's habit to write poetry in his journals in the late night or the early morning. He would often write at dawn and then go back to sleep until late morning. His waking routine took several hours. There is a good sample of that routine in "Tuesday Morn." When Allen had collected several pages of poetry in his journals, he would photocopy them and hand them to his office to perform a first typing. Peter Hale typed them and returned them promptly. Allen would make alterations by hand and return them. Sometimes this process went on through ten drafts. We kept every draft in a file folder labeled with the title of the poem. Often slight rhythmic corrections to poems would come in after Allen returned from giving poetry readings. Allen Ginsberg was one of very few poets who had the opportunity to refine the exact cadence of his lines through his frequent public readings.

One of Allen's most beautiful song lyrics was "New Stanzas for *Amazing Grace*." Allen never ignored the homeless or beggars. He was generous to a fault and could not pass an outstretched hand without leaving a coin and looking deeply into the face beyond the hand. Allen lived comfortably within his modest fame. As he walked the streets of Lower Manhattan, people would nod to him in recognition or simply say "Hi Allen!" as they passed. If they stopped to recall when they last met him or ask a question, he was patient and conversed with them. If someone came up and said, "Are you Allen Ginsberg?" he might answer, "No, but that is what I am called." Allen was always supportive of the writers he admired and who were his friends. Notice in "City Lights City" which was written for the naming ceremony of Via Ferlinghetti, Allen used the occasion to create new literary renamings of streets for all the worthy writers of his circle.

"Pastel Sentences" were written in Allen's form of American Haiku (seventeen syllables with the common haiku associational enjambment of senses but carried through on a single strophe each). These sentences were composed to accompany a set of water colors by his friend, Francesco Clemente. There was a conciliation in Allen's poems; he was commingling his worldview with its detail of causes into Buddhist mindfulness and ego urges. He continued a flirtation with children's poetry in "The Ballad of the Skeletons" which was turned into a rock 'n' roll song with Paul McCartney, Philip Glass, and Lenny Kaye collaborating musically. Gus Van Sant made a music video. Memories from East Side High, Paterson, are explored in "You know what I'm saying?" Allen remembered the songs of his childhood ("Popular Tunes"). One day he walked around the loft trying to find his scarf. He sang a little ditty about the lost scarf, which became "Gone Gone Gone": a poem about loss, which was read at a Buddhist service the day after Allen's death.

⁜

Allen was unsteady on his feet, hesitant in his step, and exhausted in his frame. He had to fly the shuttle to Boston to see his cardiologist. I sensed that, for the first time, he didn't have the energy to fly by himself. "Allen, I'll go with you," I reassured him in the early twilight of a late February afternoon. He protested that it was not necessary. I insisted and he gave in happily.

I carried my bag and his. He shuffled with me. In the taxi to LaGuardia Airport, Allen asked for his book bag. The taxi was dark, only lit by the street lamps whisking by in an alternating stream. As the vehicle sped between lanes, I felt my stomach rise up to my throat and stick there. Allen said, "Listen to this. I started it last night!" He was laughing and cracking up. He searched in his journal and found the scrawled poem. It started:

> When I die
> I don't care what happens to my body
> throw ashes in the air, scatter 'em in the East River
> bury an urn in Elizabeth New Jersey, B'nai Israel Cemetery
> But I want a big funeral

I wanted the cab ride to be over. I didn't want to hear the poem, but it got funnier and funnier. He was almost in hysterics as he listed what all his myriad boyfriends would say at his funeral. He wanted to know if I could add any lines. I suggested that women would all say, "He never did remember my name."

On the shuttle, Allen fell into a deep sleep. I stared at the deep lines in his face. He seemed so far away. I thought he might be dead. But at the beginning of our descent, he jerked awake, grabbed his notebook, scribbled for about two minutes, and read me this American sentence: "My father dying of Cancer, head drooping, 'Oy kindelach.'"

Allen's health continued to deteriorate. Poems were being written so fast that we could not keep up with them. Weeks after the trip to Boston, Allen entered Beth Israel Hospital in New York City. One of the doctors in the Emergency Room handed Allen a poem he had written seeking Allen's improvements. Allen obliged and was pleased as he confided in me that it was "a much stronger poem now." In the hospital, Allen asked for a copy of *Mother Goose.* I brought my children's Rackham edition. "Starry Rhymes" injected pure beauty into the simple rhymes. The poetry of late March 1997 reflected Allen's lively mind balancing the primary hospital bodily events and his childhood innocence so long overridden in the need to grow up fast in a dysfunctional family.

Although we are unsure that Allen had finished with the rhymes dated March 24, 1997, we include them as exemplar of the pure, supple child Allen slipped in and out of in the late stages of liver cancer. "Dream" resolves contradictions inherent in his long love affair with Peter Orlovsky and remained the last poem written before the fatal diagnosis of liver cancer. After being told of the massive metastasized cancer within him, Allen Ginsberg only completed one poem in his final week of life. "Things I'll Not Do (Nostalgias)" is the only poem that Allen did not have a chance to proof and amend before his death. The poem is a compendium of farewells, with honest regrets and true Buddhist ability to let go. Allen was sad to leave the world, but he was also exhilarated.

Besides calling friends to take leave, and extract a few promises, he wrote a final political letter to President Clinton. He prefaces his note with, "Enclosed some recent political poems." Allen lapsed into his death coma before he could select the poems.

In preparing *Death & Fame*, Peter Hale, Bill Morgan, and myself have honored Allen's insistence on chronology and notes. We have included each poem as Allen fashioned it. We suspect that some of the short verse would be further revised and combined. These are the final poetry breaths—no more Allen Ginsberg. When Allen died many people felt as if a large hole gaped in their lives. Allen left many writings and songs to fill that hole. With *Death & Fame*, we find the circle will be unbroken.

Bob Rosenthal
July 7, 1998

NOTES

(p. 1)   "New Democracy Wish List"
Ryan White Care Act—A federal program designed to provide support services for people with HIV/AIDS. The act was named for youth Ryan White, a hemophiliac who had contracted HIV through blood transfusion. His battle to return to school helped advance the rights of people living with AIDS.

SLA—Savings & Loan Association, a 1980's Federal program to bail out bankrupted savings & loan banks resulted in much mis-use and corruption.

Hand & Lavoro Bank Thuggery—Lavoro: Banca Nazionale del Lavoro.

(p. 4)   "Peace in Bosnia-Herzegovina"
Thich Nhat Hanh—(b. 1926) Zen monk, exiled from Vietnam, heads a retreat community in the south of France. Authored over seventy-five books.

Sakharov—Andrei Sakharov (1921–1989) Russian engineer and humanist, first known as "father of the Soviet Hydrogen Bomb" but soon realized radioactivity's hazards and in a series of articles confronted the Soviet government. In 1975, he was awarded the Nobel Peace Prize.

Albert Schweitzer—(1875–1965) Theologian, minister, medical missionary in Gabon, Organist, awarded the Nobel Peace prize in 1952. Schweitzer was in fact Sartre's cousin, though Sartre referred to him as "uncle Al."

(p. 6)   "After the Party"
Coemergent Wisdom—A key term in Vajrayana Buddhism referring to the simultaneous arising of samsara and nirvana, naturally giving birth to wisdom.

(p. 7)   "After Olav H. Hauge"
Olav H. Hauge—Norwegian poet (1908–1994). Trained as a gardener, his work was inspired by the natural world.

Bodø—Second largest city of northern Norway, just inside the Arctic Circle.

(p. 12)   "Tuesday Morn"
Exquisite Corpse—Literary Journal, edited by poet Andrei Codrescu.
Peter's flown—Peter Orlovsky
Sawang's . . . confirmation—*Sawang*: Previous title for Sakyong Mipham
Rinpoche (see note, page 108). *Confirmation*: Or enthronement in Tibetan
Buddhism, it is the formal recognition of an incarnation.

(p. 14)   "God"
Willendorf Venus—Late Stone-Age limestone statuette of Venus, found
near the village of Willendorf, Austria.
39 patriarchs—In Chinese and Zen Buddhism, patriarch is the founder
of a school and his successors. In some accounts lineages are traced back to
28 original Patriarchs in India, and many more in China, although never as a
group of 39—. It's likely the Author remembered incorrectly here.

(p. 16)   "Excrement"
Polyhymnia—Polyhymnia (Polymnia) is one of the nine muses; some-
times considered the muse of Sacred Poetry.

(p. 21)   "Pastel Sentences"
The author had worked out a series of 108 seventeen syllable sentences
describing individual pastel paintings by Francesco Clemente. With a copy of
the catalogue, he continued to polish them as he traveled on. Included here
are the sentences that the Author felt could stand alone without accompany-
ing images.

(p. 27)   "Is About"
muggles—Hipster term for marijuana cigarette.

(p. 29)   "The Ballad of the Skeletons"
Yahoo—From Swift's *Gulliver's Travels*: A member of a race of brutes
who have all the human vices, hence a boorish, crass, or stupid person.
Heritage Policy—Heritage Foundation: Conservative foundation think
tank, often thwarting NEA projects, opposing social welfare programs and
favoring strict FCC restrictions on "indecent" language. In their own words
"One of the nations largest public policy research organizations."
NAFTA—North American Free Trade Agreement, passed by President
Clinton and Congress over objections of many labor and environmental
groups concerned about lowered workplace and ecological safeguards.
Maquiladora—Foreign-owned factories operating on the Mexican side
of the U.S./Mexican border producing goods mainly for the U.S. market.

GATT—General Agreement on Tariffs and Trade.
I.M.F.—International Monetary Fund.

(p. 35)   "Bowel Song"
Bam—Seed syllable for Vajrayogini, one of the Author's principal Tibetan Buddhist practices.

(p. 39)   "Power"
Yuga—As in kaliyuga, Sanskrit for "age," as in the dark age.

(p. 40)   "Anger"
Carolyn—Carolyn Cassady.

(p. 41)   "Multiple Identity Questionnaire"
chela—Sanskrit term, literally "servant," though often used as the general word for a student, as in a spiritual student seeking guidance from a teacher.
neti neti—"Not this, not this." Vedantic process of discrimination by negation.
Maya—Sanskrit term in Buddhism meaning "deception, illusion, appearance," the continually changing impermanent phenomenal world of appearances and forms of illusion or deception which the unenlightened mind takes as the only reality.

(p. 42)   "Don't Get Angry with Me"
Chödok Tulku—Gelugpa school Tibetan Lama friend of Gelek Rinpoche, he was a guest speaker at a summer retreat attended by the Author. Because of nervousness or difficulty with English, he repeatedly interjected, "Don't get angry with me." The Author found it funny and innocent and wrote this poem during the lecture.
Tila, Mila, Marpa, Naro—Said here in prayer form, it is short for Tilopa, Milarepa, Marpa, Naropa (Gampopa). The line of saints or Mahasidhas of Kagupa lineage of Tibetan Buddhism.

(p. 46)   "Reverse the rain of Terror . . ."
Rocky Flats—Rockwell Corporation Nuclear Facility's Plutonium Bomb trigger factory, near Boulder, Colorado. Starting in the late '70s, the Author joined in many protests against the plant. In 1989 the FBI investigated the site, confirmed careless handling of radioactive materials, suspended activity there and subsequently shut it down, but only after a $2 billion failed attempt to get the plant back on line. Cleanup will continue into the next millennium.

(p. 48) "Sending Message"

General Rios-Montt—Efrain Rios-Montt (b. 1926), Guatemalan dictator, rose to power in a 1982 coup lasting seventeen months. Claiming himself a "Born-Again" Christian reformer and backed by President Reagan, his campaigns were responsible for the destruction of native villages and the killing of tens of thousands of natives.

700 Club—Televangelist cable talk show, Christian Broadcasting Networks's Flagship program, founded by Pat Robertson.

(p. 55) "Happy New Year Robert & June"

Robert & June—Robert Frank, June Lief.

(p. 56) "Diamond Bells"

Hayagriva—One of the eight fierce protective deities, identified by a horse's head in Tibetan Buddhist iconology.

(p. 58) "Waribashi"

See "Roots of Rain Forest Destruction," Khor Kok Pen, *Third World Resurgence*, no. 4, December 1990 (Malaysia, Third World Network), paraphrased in *The Debt Boomerang*, Susan George, 1992 (London, Pluto Press with Transnational Institute).

(p. 68) "Death & Fame"

Trungpa Vajracharya—*Vajracharya*: In Tibetan Buddhism, Mantrayana-style meditation practice master. *Trungpa*: Chögyam Trungpa, Rinpoche (1939–1987), the Author's first meditation master (1971–1987), founder of Naropa institute and Shambhala centers, author of *Cutting Through Spiritual Materialism* and *First Thought Best Thought*, with introduction by Allen Ginsberg, 1984, both published by Shambhala Publications, Boston.

Gelek Rinpoche—Kyabje or Ngawang Gelek Rinpoche (b. 1939), friend and teacher to the Author, he is the founder of Jewel Heart Tibetan Buddhist centers. A refugee in India since 1959, where he gave up monastic life to better serve the Tibetan Buddhist lay community, in the late '70s he was directed by tutors to the Dalai Lama to begin teaching Western students. He currently resides in Ann Arbor, Michigan.

Sakyong Mipham Rinpoche—(b. 1962) The lineage holder of the Buddhist and Shambhala meditation traditions brought from Tibet by his father and teacher, Chögyam Trungpa Rinpoche. He is the leader of the international Shambhala community based in Halifax, Nova Scotia.

Satchitananda Swami—Sri Swami Satchidananda, founder of Integral Yoga Institute. Came to the United States from India 1966.

Dehorahava Baba—A yogi the Author met at the Ganges River across from Benares in 1963.

Karmapa XVI—(1924–1981) Sixteenth lama head of Milarepa lineage, Kagupa order of Tibetan Buddhism.

Dudjom Rinpoche—(1904–1987) Former lama head of Nyingmapa "old school" Tibetan teachings, founded by Padmasambhava.

Katigiri Roshi—Dainin Katagiri-Roshi (1928–1990), first Abbot of the Minnesota Zen Meditation Center in Minneapolis. Came to the United States from Japan in 1963. Taught and practiced in California and also assisted Suzuki-roshi at the San Francisco Zen Center.

Suzuki Roshi—Shunryu Suzuki-roshi: Zen master of the Soto Lineage. Came to the United States in 1958 as head of the Japanese Soto sect in San Francisco, where he established a Zen Center. He built Zen Mountain Center at Tassajara Springs, the first Zen monastery in America. His Dharma heir is Richard Baker.

Baker Roshi—Richard Baker, Roshi, Abbot, head teacher, and founder of the Dharma Sangha centers, Crestone, Colorado, and Germany.

Whalen Roshi—Zenshin Philip Whalen (b. 1923), poet friend associated with the Beat Generation, now an ordained Zen Buddhist priest, he is Abbot of the Hartford Street Zen Center, San Francisco.

Daido Loori Roshi—John Daido Loori, Abbot of Zen Mountain Monastery in Mt. Tremper, New York, and the founder/director of the Mountains and Rivers Order. Master in Rinzai and Soto lines of Zen Buddhism. Dharma heir of Hakuyu Taizen Maezumi Roshi.

Kapleau Roshi—Philip Kapleau Roshi, Zen master, studied Zen in Japan, founded the Rochester Zen Center in 1966, author of many books on Zen practice.

Lama Tarchin—Nyingmapa school Tibetan Lama, founded the Vajrayana Foundation, Santa Cruz, California, at the request of HH Dudjom Rinpoche.

(p. 71) "Sexual Abuse"
See article "Sexual Abuse Bill Targets Clergy," Mark Mueller, *Boston Herald* (February 21, 1997).

(p. 74) "Half Asleep"
Almora—Town in Uttar Pradesh state of Northern India, near the foothills of the Himalayas.

(p. 89) "Thirty State Bummers"
Idi Amin—Idi Amin Dada Oumee (b. 1925), president and dictator of Uganda from 1971–1979, responsible for the killing of 300,000 tribal Ugandans.

General Mobutu—Joseph Mobutu (1930–1997), president and dictator of Zaire from 1965–1991, supported by Western powers.

Mr. Allende—Salvador Allende Gossens (1908–1973), Popularly elected Democratic Socialist President of Chile, overthrown by a military coup supported by the CIA.

Pinochet—Augusto Pinochet Ugarte (b. 1915), president of Chile following the death of Allende.

D'Aubuisson—Roberto D'Aubuisson Arrieta, Death Squad Leader of Arena Party in El Salvador.

Pat Robertson—Conservative Baptist minister and television talk show host who ran for president in 1988.

Rios-Montt—(See note, p. 108.)

Col. North—Oliver L. North, Jr. (b. 1943), U.S. Marine Colonel and a key figure in the Iran-Contra affair.

Aristide—Jean-Bertrand Aristide (b. 1951), the first democratically elected leader of Haiti from 1990–1991 and 1994–1995.

Cedras—Lt. Gen. Raoul Cedras, Haitian military ruler who overthrew Aristide in 1991.

Fujimori—Alberto Fujimori (b. 1938), president of Peru.

United Fruits—Corporation that controlled much of the Central American fruit market and now part of United Brands Company. United Fruit Company's law firm, Sullivan and Cromwell, had employed State Secretary Dulles, whose brother, Allen, heading the CIA, coordinated the 1954 then-covert overthrow of Jacob Arbenz, elected president of Guatemala. The event is notorious throughout Latin America as a mid-twentieth-century example of "banana republic" repression by North American imperium. By 1980, the U.S.-trained Guatemalan military had reportedly killeed 10 percent of jungle Indian population as part of a "pacification" program to "create a favorable business climate." (See note: Rios-Montt.)

Mosaddeq—Mohammad Mosaddeq (1880–1967), Democratically elected Iranian premier from 1951–1953 who nationalized Western oil holdings.

Pol Pot—(1928–1998), Prime Minister of Cambodia from 1976–1979 and former leader of the Khmer Rouge.

Sihanook—Norodom Sihanook, Prime Minister since 1955 and crowned king of Cambodia in 1993 for the second time.

(p. 98) "Things I'll Not Do (Nostalgias)"

Kashi—Known now as Benares, a city in northern India, mentioned in ancient Buddhist writings.

Manikarnika ghat—Benares, India; steps near the river where corpses are burned.

Jagganath, Lord—Lord Jagganath is the form under which the Hindu god Krishna is worshipped in Puri, a town in eastern India.

Birbhum—A district in West Bengal state, northeastern India, home of nineteenth-century holy fool, Khaki Baba (see below).

Khaki Baba—North Bengali (Birbhum area), nineteenth-century saint who, dressed in khaki loincloth, is pictured sometimes sitting surrounded by canine friends and protectors.

Philip—Philip Glass, American composer.

Sunil—Sunil Ganguly, Indian poet-friend.

Choudui Chowh Nimtallah—Calcutta neighborhood where the Author lived in the summer of 1962, near the burning ghats.

Soco Chico—Square in the medina, Tangiers, where outdoor cafes were popular with the Author, William S. Burroughs, and Paul Bowles.

Paul B.—Paul Bowles, American writer living in Tangier.

Baluchistan—Baluchistan province in Pakistan, bordered by Afghanistan on the north and Iran on the west.

Dunhuang—Pinyin Dunhuang, city in western Kansu Sheng province, China.

Buba—(Yiddish) *Grandmother* Rebecca Ginsberg was Allen Ginsberg's grandmother, buried in this cemetery.

INDEX OF TITLES
AND FIRST LINES

Poem titles appear in *italics*.

ABOUT THE AUTHOR

ALLEN GINSBERG was born in 1926 in Newark, New Jersey, a son of Naomi Ginsberg and lyric poet Louis Ginsberg. In 1956 he published his signal poem "Howl," one of the most widely read and translated poems of the century. A member of the American Academy of Arts and Letters, awarded the medal of Chevalier de l'Ordre des Arts et Lettres by the French Minister of Culture in 1993, and cofounder of the Jack Kerouac School of Disembodied Poetics at Naropa Institute, the first accredited Buddhist college in the Western world, Allen Ginsberg died in 1997.